Chef Fritz and His City

Also by Samuel Young

Psychic Children (1978)

Chef Fritz and His City

My Education in the Master's Kitchen

Samuel Young

Terra Nova Books

SANTA FE, NEW MEXICO

Terra Nova Books

Published by Terra Nova Books, Santa Fe, New Mexico.
www.TerraNovaBooks.com

ISBN 978-1-938288-37-1

*T*HANKS, FIRST OF ALL, to Maggie Simmons, my editor-in-chief at *Travel Holiday*, who prompted my initial visit to Fritz Blank's Deux Cheminées. Thanks to Blank's innumerable friends and colleagues who shared my admiration for the polymath chef and helped with this book in various ways. I am particularly indebted to Patricia Arcaro, Nick Malgieri, and Nancy Nicholas for generous assistance. Thanks also to Oliver Benson, Brad Goldfarb, and Nick Paumgarten for advice and encouragement. And to John Berendt, my colleague from *Lampoon* days, special thanks for cogent observations and for laughing in the right places. To Lynne Farrington, curator of printed books at the University of Pennsylvania's Annenberg Rare Book and Manuscript Library, my gratitude for making time for me in her crushing schedule. Thanks to Marty and Scott Gerber, editor and publisher, for being the right people at the right time. And to my wife, Risa Benson, thanks without end for good advice and timely goading, to say nothing of the tango instruction; let's trust in the pet saying of Fritz's dear friend, Esther Press McManus: "The longer it takes, the better it is."

Contents

*Chef Fritz's holiday card (with hand-drawn elves). Inside message,
"Here's hoping that your holidays are filled with Epicurean Pleasures."
1998*

Philadelphia From the Ashes

*T*HERE WAS A GLORIOUS MOMENT in American history when Philadelphia was the nation's capital and the hub of the New World. Only London and Dublin in the English-speaking sphere had more people and influence. But then the federal government went south to a fen by the Potomac River, and the money business drifted to New York. Just in my lifetime, Philadelphia has declined from the third most populous American city to the sixth, and the number it sends to the U.S. House of Representatives has dwindled from seven to three. Like some other great cities of diminished influence (Kyoto, Fes, and Vienna come to mind), Philadelphia suffers from wounded pride, causing the civic mood to be prickly and insular.

The long decline was most evident after the Second World War. In the summer of 1948, when both the Republican and Democratic parties held their nominating conventions in a splendid Art Deco hall near the University of Pennsylvania, the city was surprised and embarrassed to discover a shortage of hotel rooms. From 1856, the year the new Republican Party held its first national nominating convention in the Musical Fund Society Hall, to 1948, Philadelphia hosted the presidential candidate selection seven times. But after the hotel fiasco of 1948, there would be no political conventions in the city for more than fifty years. Yet in 1948, the city was still a powerhouse. The Pennsylvania Railroad, in magnificent headquarters on Thirtieth Street, was the nation's principal transportation enterprise. The Curtis Publishing Company, occupying a citadel of its own on Independence Square, dominated the nation's magazine publishing with the *Saturday Evening Post, Ladies' Home Journal,* and *Holiday.* We know what happened to *them:* Travel by automobile and air doomed the railroads, and magazine readers became television viewers. (The putative creator of television, Philo T. Farnsworth, developed his invention in the 1930s while living in Philadelphia and working for the Philadelphia Storage Battery Company, or Philco, but his brainchild was wrested from his grasp by a New Yorker, David Sarnoff of RCA.)

On top of those reversals, a plan to build the United Nations headquarters in the city died on the vine. According to Mark Bernstein, writing in *Philadelphia* magazine, "Few people remember today, but Philadelphia's bid to be selected as the permanent headquarters of the United Nations came within a weekend of success. On December 11, 1946, the day the vote was scheduled to be taken, the *New York Times'* front page declared Philadelphia the probable choice. Adlai Stevenson, then a member of the American delegation, assured the city's sponsors they were a lock. Eventually, of course, Philadelphia was snookered by New York, as Philadelphia always is."

The snookering, Bernstein said, was accomplished by a last-minute deal—and a donation of $8.5 million—engineered by John D. Rockefeller Jr. and his son Nelson. The New York bid offered "less land, worth less money, in a crowded and rundown part of town," but "despite considerable grumbling" among United Nations planners, the deal went through.

Even before its hapless decline, Philadelphia was becoming the butt of jokes. The movie comedian and native son William Claude Dukenfield, better known as W.C. Fields, famously damned the city with scant praise by proposing as his epitaph, "I'd rather be in Philadelphia." An apocryphal contest awarded the winner a week's stay in Philadelphia, the runner-up two weeks. A Washington grand dame is said to have remarked, "The Gay Nineties are still alive in Philadelphia: All the men are gay and all the women are ninety." And there was the infamous dig, "I visited Philadelphia, but it was closed."

That last remark bore some truth. In the 1950s, when Dwight and Mamie Eisenhower lived in the White House and Poppy Cannon's *The Can Opener Cook Book* was a popular kitchen reference, Philadelphia had perhaps three restaurants of much ambition, and two of those were in hotels. Philadelphians typically ate at home or in their clubs. A stranger in town with a taste for something less prosaic than Salisbury steak and a glass of warm rosé could be in trouble. Even the Automat was in decline. For more than fifty years, the coin-operated cafeterias of Joseph Horn and Augustin Hardart had provided comfort food of good quality to Philadelphians and New Yorkers, but now the Automats were showing their age, and Americans' food tastes were changing.

Behind the scenes, Philadelphians' love of good food had not died out, for in its early heyday the city that was established on principles of Quaker tolerance embraced Epicureanism and the pursuit of happiness at table. It was the acknowledged capital of American gastronomy, sustained by ocean, rivers, and heartlands, and ships foraging from the West Indies to China. In 1839, Frances Gund, the author of *Aristocracy in America*, declared, "Philadelphians have more taste and have the best cooks in the United States." Today, if one can say that New Yorkers are money hungry and Washingtonians are power hungry, then Philadelphians are merely hungry. Food is their joy and solace.

It was hunger, in fact, that got the city out of the doldrums. As Europe recovered from World War II and Philadelphians, along with other Americans, began to travel there, cooks and restaurant patrons raised their sights. At a country inn outside the city, a kitchen crusader named Wallis Callahan hid the catsup bottle from his patrons, sometimes banned steak from his menu ("too tame"), and dared to serve *crevette rémoulade, coquilles St. Jacques,* and *rognons de veau.* Word got out. Excited Philadelphians made the forty-mile trip to Callahan's Coventry Forge Inn. Out of the inn's kitchen came an ambitious hand named Peter von Starck, who made his way to l'Ousteau de Beaumanière, in Provence, where he was a *saucier* and *poissonier*. There von Starck met Georges Perrier, a rising star from Lyons, and enticed him to open a French restaurant together in Philadelphia. The restaurant, La Panetière, was a hit, though Perrier and von Starck parted company after three years and Perrier went on to create his own success, the durable, *raffiné*, and expensive Le Bec-Fin.

Inspired, uncompromising, choleric, and tireless, Perrier, in effect, willed Philadelphia out of its apathy and self-pity. "I like this city because it feels provincial, not like a big huge city in France," he once said. "Still, you have to sacrifice your life to be successful in the restaurant—eighteen, nineteen, twenty, twenty-four hours a day, or more." When Craig Claiborne of the *New York Times* declared Le Bec-Fin to be one of the finest restaurants in America, Philadelphians stood straighter. Today, any hungry epicure, resident, or visitor has no end of options. In fact, city life has improved to the extent that significant numbers of New Yorkers have moved to Philadelphia, preferring to live there, at less expense, and commute to work in Manhattan, along with hundreds of Philadelphians who have been doing so for years.

In the 1990s, I was one of those commuters. *Holiday,* the fine old travel magazine started by the Curtis Publishing Company, my first employer, had moved to New York decades before and merged with the magazine *Travel.* For a number of palmy years, I was an editor and writer for *Travel Holiday,* making the daily rattling Amtrak ride between Philadelphia and New York in return for the occasional writing trip to destinations popular at the time: Morocco, for one, and Santorini, Martinique, and Kyoto. One fateful assignment was to tour my own town in the guise of a visitor. The American Society of Travel Agents, which customarily met in places like Lisbon and Bangkok, would be holding its annual convention in Philadelphia. This was a significant event for American tourism, and *Travel Holiday* wanted a cover story about the host city.

I had lived for years in a northwest corner of the city, first in Chestnut Hill and then in Mount Airy, but I was not, strictly speaking, a Philadelphian by birth. I grew up thirty miles to the southwest, in the farmlands of Chester County. Yet family ties to the city were strong. My father and uncle practiced law there, commuting each day by rail. My mother's father was born in Philadelphia, the descendant of a Welsh Quaker who had sailed from England with William Penn. Grandfather Howell spent his early years in the city, working in a grand domed bank on Broad Street and sculling on the Schuylkill River. My father's father worked in the city as well. A grandee of the Pennsylvania Railroad, he cut an elegant figure in a bowler and bespoke suit with a carnation in the lapel.

He sometimes took me on trips in a private railroad car, and before departure would tour me around his work domain, subordinates salaaming along our way. My Cousin Margaret, a kind spinster, took me to the great cinema palaces of the day, the Mastbaum and the Randolph, since demolished. I have forgotten the movies we saw but remember the opulence of the surroundings, as grand as any over-budget Hollywood set. And Aunt Ann, my mother's sister, took me to Friday matinee performances of the Philadelphia Orchestra at the Academy of Music, a neo-Baroque extravaganza fashioned after La Scala in Milan. Our seats were among the fur-wearing matrons in a fashionable part of the hall, but Aunt Ann would indulge my wish to visit the high tiers, from where I could watch the tympanist bang away. Philadelphia was my spectacle and playground.

Over the years, of course, the bright city of my childhood acquired blight and tarnish, in my adult view. But as I toured the city for *Travel Holiday*, I tried to put aside my old perspectives and see the city through what Buddhists call "beginner eyes." Like a householder who, expecting guests, looks around his quarters and suddenly sees clutter, I recognized what an old curiosity shop Philadelphia is. "We are curious about the world beyond our boundaries," I wrote, "and have stuffed our museums, parlors, attics, and shops with the trophies and detritus of travel." As a colleague wrote of Istanbul, Philadelphia is a city that has never been properly sacked. It is a den of nesters and collectors. I was intrigued, and compelled to look further into the nature of the town from which our nation grew.

In the Chef's Kitchen

*T*HE CHEF, ALL BILLOWY IN WHITE, navigated his dining room like a ship under sail, greeting the few customers. When he arrived at our table, he docked himself in the extra chair and let out a great sigh.

"One snowflake falls, everyone stays home. No customers. No delivery trucks."

Months after my article on Philadelphia had appeared in *Travel Holiday*, the city was recovering from a winter cold snap that had put the region into a kind of cryogenic suspension. When the cold abated, my wife and I resolved to raise our spirits by venturing out to Deux Cheminées, a restaurant well regarded in our region but one we had never tried. It was just the ticket: remarkable food and wine served in the not-too-formal surroundings of the former Princeton Club. The waiters wore their tuxedos without pomposity, and fires blazed cheerfully in several fireplaces. We did not want our meal to end, but when it did, we were consoled by the unexpected arrival of the chef.

Visiting tables is a custom the Troisgros family introduced in the 1950s at their restaurant near Lyon. Visiting tables to grumble, as Chef Fritz Blank seemed in the mood to do that evening, might be peculiar to Philadelphia, a place where grousing is endemic.

"You're in a cruel line of work, Chef," I said, wanting to commiserate.

Blank leaned forward. His ruddy skin and the short English toque he wore low on his brow gave him a fierce aspect, but his blue eyes were merry.

"Don't get me started," he said, forgetting that he had been ranting about this and that for several minutes. "Do you know the saying about Philadelphia's four rivers?"

We did not.

"Well, there's the Delaware, right?"

"Yes."

"And the Schuylkill?"

"Yes."

"And the Wissahickon?"

The Wissahickon was really a creek, not a river, but we didn't quibble.

"And the fourth. . . ." Blank raised a corner of his apron and pretended to wipe a tear from his cheek. "The fourth river," he said with quavering voice, "is the tears of the chefs!"

We laughed. Blank raised himself out of the chair, waved jauntily, and moved on.

Several months after our evening at Deux Cheminées, I shed real tears of my own when *Reader's Digest* sold *Travel Holiday* to a European company and most of my colleagues on staff were sacked. I did not have the stomach to work for the new regime, so what to do? As it happened, my wife's business, Risa Benson Knitwear, which operated from our house, was growing fast, and Risa's time was consumed with the minutiae of patterns, schedules, yarn orders, and managing her assistants. What if I learned to cook so I could take over in the kitchen?

As if on cue, a circular came in the mail from the University of Pennsylvania, listing continuing-education studies for the fall term. Sharing a page with "Soil, Mulch, and Compost Techniques" was a course titled "In the Chef's Kitchen." It involved three Monday-morning sessions. "Let your creative culinary plans begin in the award-winning restaurant of Master Chef Fritz Blank," the blurb said. "Participants will observe the preparation of three simple French meals before sitting down to a sumptuous lunch at the chef's table. Enrollment limited to 20."

The prospect of learning from Chef Blank in his restaurant kitchen was exciting but also unnerving. Until then, Risa and I had improvised together at the stove. On my own, I could scramble eggs and make an adequate risotto, but I had scant understanding of the everyday business of buying and preparing food. Risa was an experienced and often-inspired cook who had made a pilgrimage in her 20s to the culinary shrines of France. And she had spent many months with her Paumgarten cousins in Vienna (her father had immigrated to the U.S. in the 1920s), cooking with them and browsing the city's *konditorei*.

But she did not like to plan meals, had little patience at the stove, and could not abide consulting a recipe unless it involved baking. Her favored implement was the wok, volcanic catchall for anything at hand: peppers, chicken, tofu, zucchini, eggplant, snow peas, broccoli. I would chop, she would furiously stir and scorch, raising oily clouds that set off the smoke alarm and made us throw open doors and windows. The result was usually delicious, for though she cooked with a hash slinger's abandon, she had an epicure's judgment. Could I rise to that level? I dawdled over the application to Chef Blank's course.

Some weeks later, I learned that WHYY, the city's major public television station, was raising money by presenting live cooking demonstrations by the "Great Chefs of Philadelphia," Fritz Blank among them. I wanted to look him over once more, and talked my way into the show. At the appointed hour, in the gloom of the WHYY studios, I saw a stout man emerge from a shadowy corridor pushing a metal cart. On it lay a long knife and a fish the size of a small child. The fish was quite dead, but one of its eyes seemed fixed on me, beseeching. As the man drew near, I noticed his Mephistophelean beard, the tattoos on his arms, the ring in his left ear. He wore a white jacket, striped pants, moccasins without socks, and a toque that looked like a butcher's cap. He reminded me of the taciturn Rhinelanders photographed by August Sander in the 1920s and '30s. It was Blank. I was sure he did not remember me from the dinner months before, but when he reached me, he paused and held out a jar.

"Have one," he said.

Inside the jar, flesh-colored globules bobbed in a ruddy liquid, as though embalmed.

"Um. What are they?"

"Cherries soaked for a year in Calvados."

"Oh. Thanks."

The Calvados allayed the gloom of the surroundings. Between live demonstrations, the station was airing its regular lineup of cooking shows on tape. Just now, on a big monitor, Jacques Pépin chopped and chattered while Julia Child hovered at his shoulder.

A tall Eurasian chef walked over to us.

He wore jeans and lizard-skin cowboy boots. The stitching on his jacket told us he was Philippe Chin, of Chanterelles. He and Blank hugged.

"Allo, Freetz," Chin said. "Bluefish, eh?"

"I'm using a Hungarian recipe for carp, called *ràcponty*," Blank said. "I'll do *tomaten salat* and my grandmother's German potato salad. Breadcake, too, if I have time: *gâteau d'Allarde.*"

"That's a lot for twenty minutes. Better cook fast." Chin sauntered off, and Blank put on a big white apron and wheeled his cart to the TV-set kitchen where a counter, cook-top, and overhead mirror faced several big cameras. Beyond the cameras were the telephone banks where volunteers received callers' pledges. The volunteers had gone on break between the live segments, and now they were returning as Blank busied himself in the rudimentary kitchen.

Suddenly he was toiling back my way, heading for the staging room.

"I'm in deep shit. I don't have a saute pan."

I was horrified. It was almost airtime, and if Blank couldn't find a pan, perhaps a hundred thousand food enthusiasts would witness his disgrace. With scarcely thirty seconds to spare, he returned, pan in hand, looking unfazed. The studio lights went up, a hostess introduced him, and the demonstration began. For twenty minutes Blank fluidly cooked, instructed the TV audience, and chatted up the hostess. When the segment was over, the studio lights went down and the completed meal was removed to a side room where it was set upon by the staff. I filled a plate and found myself a chair. Blank did not eat but eased into a chair nearby.

"I probably tried to do too much," he said.

"It looked fine to me," I replied, "but I'm someone who can spend twenty minutes just opening a can."

"Do you cook?"

"Very little. I've never taken the time to learn. It was considered women's work when I was a kid."

"Same here. My mother worked full-time and still did everything in the kitchen. My father didn't lift a finger."

"You learned from your mother?"

"No. My mother hated to cook. I learned from my grandmother, an old-school German who raised chickens and kept all kinds of preserved food in her cellar. Sauerkraut, pickled cucumbers, green tomatoes. This was just across the river from here, in Pennsauken. It's all gone now, but there were fields and creeks and ponds, and we lived off it all. We ate muskrats, snapping turtles, squirrels, quail, rabbits, sunfish, catfish, pheasant, mourning doves. Good eating, too. We picked blackberries, fox grapes, elderberries, and chokecherries, and made jams and jellies. Everyone had a victory garden in the backyard, and fruit trees. Nut trees, too. A lot of families raised chickens, ducks, rabbits."

"I grew up in the country, too," I said, feeling vaguely competitive. "We had a big victory garden during the war, and my mother pickled and made preserves. I remember drinking raw milk from the dairy up the road."

"Yeah, our milk was raw, too," Blank said. "It came by horse-drawn wagon, chilled with blocks of ice. It's hard to imagine now. You know, we had no running hot water in our house until I was thirteen."

He had me there.

Soon Blank got up to leave. He said his restaurant was overrun with out-of-towners who had come for the Cézanne exhibit at the Philadelphia Museum of Art.

"We're booked up and short-handed. August is usually slow, so I let a lot of the staff go on vacation. Who knew?"

He shook hands all around, then rolled his cart down the corridor to the back door. I left by the front of the WHYY building and stood for a moment on Sixth Street, facing the park at the north end of Independence Mall. Through the canopy of trees, I could just make out the U.S. Mint over on Fifth Street, and the burial ground where Benjamin Franklin, I liked to imagine, was keeping an eye on the nation's coinage production.

Philadelphia summers can be hot and sultry, but this late afternoon was merely hot, with a saving breeze. I walked south past the Liberty Bell pavilion to Chestnut Street, where the lowering sun animated the old bricks of Independence Hall. A half-block farther down Sixth, I stopped to look at the marble arcades of the Curtis Center, the old headquarters of Curtis Publishing. In 1961, just out of college, I'd landed a junior editor's job at its *Saturday Evening Post.* When I came to work in the morning, I walked past *The Dream Garden,* a glass mosaic based on a painting by Maxfield Parrish and executed by the Louis Comfort Tiffany Studios. (There were murals by Parrish on the top floor as well.) An elevator operator, wearing white gloves, conveyed me up to the office floors where communications between departments traveled by pneumatic tube and a smiling woman and her armed escort toured the halls each week to deliver our pay, in cash. When the Curtis magazines came off the presses in the same enormous building, they were trundled across town to the main post office on electric wagons that moved at the speed of an indolent pedestrian. But the 1960s were upon us. Months after I started work at Curtis, the company moved its editors to an aluminum-clad skyscraper on Fifth Avenue in New York, and I went along for a time.

Now I walked past the old Curtis building, crossed Washington Square, and went west on Locust. This had been the usual route home to my first apartment, a creaking walkup just off Locust, between Thirteenth and Broad. Today I was going only as far as Ninth, where I had parked. Before I reached my car, I stopped to peer at the Musical Fund Society Hall, built for the appreciation of music in 1824. The city has so many "oldests" and "firsts" in the nation that it hardly seemed remarkable that this was America's oldest surviving music hall, that Jenny Lind, the Swedish soprano, had sung here and Dickens and Thackeray had lectured. In 1856 a coalition of Northern Whigs and Democrats opposed to slavery held its first national nominating convention in the hall. The Republicans, as they called themselves, selected John C. Fremont of California as their candidate. He failed to gain the presidency, but four years later the new party succeeded with Abraham Lincoln.

"Some cities, like wrapped boxes under Christmas trees, conceal unexpected gifts, secret delights," wrote Truman Capote in *Music for Chameleons*. "Some cities will always remain wrapped boxes, containers of riddles never to be solved." Capote was describing Fort-de-France, in the French West Indies, but I think the observation suits Philadelphia as well. If you were to continue along my old walk home on Locust to where it intersects tiny Camac Street, at the half-block between Twelfth and Thirteenth, you might understand why some say Philadelphia is a private city, a place of conundrums and hideaways.

Consider Locust itself. It is an important artery that runs for nearly six miles, generally straight across the center of the city's grid. Yet it is narrow, as urban thoroughfares go, seldom accommodating more than a lane or two of traffic. On its way from the western city limit at Cobb's Creek east to the Delaware River waterfront, it feints and fades. At the University of Pennsylvania, for example, it shrivels into a walkway. Farther on, when it reaches the west bank of the Schuylkill, there is no bridge, so you must divert north or south to cross the water that divides the city. (The Dutch name of the river suggests concealment: Hidden River. Locust resumes on the east bank, then twice fakes a dead-end when it encounters two of the city's park-like squares, Rittenhouse and Washington. The uninitiated might not guess that at both places, the street reappears on the far side of the trees.

If Locust Street tends to evade, Camac hides. Four blocks long and barely ten feet wide, it has the dimensions of an alley. But instead of back doors and garbage bins, one sees the handsome fronts of Federal-style row houses. Philadelphians have nested on tiny streets like Camac for more than two hundred years, arriving by horse or foot to dwell or meet or carouse in quarters that, to most of us, might feel cramped and out of plumb. Inexpedience, a significant number of Philadelphians feel, is a fair exchange for the coziness and privacy of places like Camac.

At the northeast corner of Locust and Camac, on my homeward walks long ago, I would pass a pair of formidable brownstone townhouses. Built some fifty years after the Camac row houses, in the gilded days of the American Centennial, they had been designed in the fanciful style of Frank Furness, Philadelphia's virtuoso of Victorian excess. I preferred the quiet neoclassical fronts on Camac, where I could imagine myself on a byway in Dublin or Edinburgh, yet I admired the big brownstones for their sportive masonry and their high front windows of leaded glass—very Castle Dracula. One window, I remember, bore a stained-glass emblem of Princeton University. Inside, I reckoned, was the Princeton Club, one of the city's many private retreats.

Three decades later, on the February night when Risa and I dined at Deux Cheminées for the first time and met Chef Blank, I had spotted the Princeton emblem in the restaurant's front window. I saw it again in the fall of that year, when I returned to the big brownstones at Locust and Camac to attend Chef Blank's cooking class. On a Monday morning in October, as I climbed the granite steps of the former Princeton Club, city workers were tidying the neighborhood after a weekend of Outfest, a gay and lesbian street fair. Inside, Blank sat at an escritoire in the front parlor. He was wearing his customary white tunic and cap-like toque, and was chatting up a dozen or so early arrivals arrayed in front of him on armchairs and settees. Behind him, the reception parlor opened into a second big parlor. Both rooms had high ceilings, fireplaces, chandeliers, chiming clocks, and oil paintings of various sizes, from small landscapes to a very large full-length portrait of a woman holding a King Charles spaniel. There was no other restaurant in the city so elaborate yet comfy, so extensively carpeted and curtained and upholstered, so reassuringly Philadelphia.

The rest of the students soon arrived. Most in the class appeared to be in their 40s or 50s, and only two were men. Some students seemed particularly chummy with the chef, and I soon learned that they had taken previous courses with him.

"I'm just back from Vienna and Budapest," Blank announced. "Louis Szathmary, a famous chef in Chicago, taught me about the food of Hungary, his birthplace, which he left as a young man, fifty years ago. In his honor I went to Grendel, the old Budapest restaurant that George Lang and Ronald Lauder have revived. It was very, very elegant, and they rolled out the red carpet for me. But I was embarrassed because the food didn't measure up to the Hungarian dishes Louis and I have made. People in Budapest told me that Hungarian cuisine lost its refinement during the Russian occupation. When I got home and reported this to Louis, he was sad but not surprised. Now I'm the sad one because Chef Louis has died, just three days ago."

Blank cheered up when he spoke of Vienna. "My favorite city. So civilized, so appealing. It's a town for walkers, like Philadelphia. In fact, Philadelphia has more than a few things in common with Vienna, but I won't say more now. It's time to go downstairs." He led us to a carpeted staircase that wound its way down to a corridor below street level. Its walls were lined with awards, photographs, and press clippings, all in neat frames. I noticed a photo of Blank with André Soltner, the chef and owner of Lutèce, in New York. In another picture, Blank stood between Louis Szathmary and the New York chef and food columnist Pierre Franey. As we proceeded down the hall, memorabilia gave way to an array of copper pots and pans. I could see the kitchen farther on, but we turned off through a doorway on our right and stepped down into a pantry. This was the staff dining room, someone told me, where lunch and supper were served on the days the restaurant was open. Shelves loaded with kitchen gear shared the walls with colorful food posters and large photographs of Blank at work.

Breakfast was set out on a butcher-block table: muffins, breads, cheese, cold cuts, and jam. In a corner at the far end of the pantry, two doorways met at a right angle, one leading to the cold storage, the other to the kitchen. No sensible designer would allow such a bottleneck for hurrying workers to negotiate, but options were limited down here where the walls were of thick nineteenth-century masonry.

We filled our plates and carried them into the kitchen, a room perhaps forty feet long and twenty feet wide. A central island of stainless steel and butcher block ran nearly the entire length, leaving aisles on either side. Chairs had been set up for us in the aisle farthest from the stoves. Chef Blank stationed himself in the other aisle, next to a soup cooker and a convection oven, his back to two soot-black Garland stoves with many burners and enormous hoods. A Chinese porcelain kitchen god presided on a shelf above the island.

I took a chair at the far end of the kitchen, next to a big wash sink and the back stairs leading to the service door and on up to a serving pantry and the dining rooms. Near me, a young man in whites was dicing kohlrabi. Chef Blank came by to inspect and ordered him—rather brusquely, I thought—to make a smaller dice. The lad appeared to be unfazed. He told me at the time that he was completing training at the Restaurant School (Philadelphia's principal school for chefs) and hoped that Deux Cheminées would hire him. "Chef Blank is so patient with beginners," he said.

We were given a list of the day's projects: *soupe aux choux-rave, escalopes de vau au Madeira, quarts de coings braisées, gratin dauphinois,* and *mange-toute vapeur.* Most of the French had been translated: kohlrabi soup, veal cutlets with Madeira sauce, braised quarters of quince. But I would have to find out for myself what *mange-tout vapeur* might be. Facing us from his side of the island, Chef Blank prepared carrots for the soup, aligning them side-by-side and removing their ends with two swift slices. Next he peeled them, not with the thin, slotted gadget familiar to me but with a Y-shaped implement called a banjo. Then he demonstrated what he called the Chinese roll cut, slicing the carrots into small triangles to create more surfaces to which sauce could adhere.

Next he arranged five quinces in a row, peeled their pale green skins, and quartered them. "This makes great jelly," he said. "Quince has been known for a long time, but it's being rediscovered." Then he gathered a fistful of parsley, thyme, and bay leaf and wrapped it with string. "This is *bouquet garni* for flavoring the soup. The bay leaves are from the tree in my quarters upstairs. I recommend growing your own. I don't say this about most plants, but bay trees have personalities. They make great companions."

Blank smeared butter in a shallow copper pan to start the *gratin dauphinois,* then rubbed in garlic cloves he had crushed with the flat of a knife. "Notice that I discard the garlic after rubbing it in the pan. In classic French cooking, no single ingredient, such as garlic, should overpower the dish. Heavily seasoned cooking belongs at home, or in bistros, but should not masquerade as *haute cuisine*. The old-time chefs would consider that disgusting."

Next Blank set up a mandoline and sliced potatoes to near transparency. He layered the slices in the copper pan, adding a mixture of heavy cream and half-and-half between the layers. "Four russet potatoes sliced this way can feed twenty. The process may seem slow, but it couldn't be simpler." He salted the potatoes, holding his hand high above the dish. "The good chefs do this. It's the proper way."

Blank put the dish of potatoes in one of the big ovens and began to slice a loin of veal. "I like electric ovens because the temperature stays more even than with gas," he said, "but I like gas burners on the top. Whatever type of oven you have, you should calibrate it by checking the temperature settings with a thermometer. Ovens have distinct personalities, like people. Most have hot spots. Some are just unfriendly."

As Blank chattered on, it was difficult to believe he was simultaneously making lunch for close to two dozen of us. He seemed to produce food in the casual way one of my grandmothers knitted sweaters while telling stories. Now he was citing Escoffier's rule for combining dairy-based liquids with other liquids. One must be hot—it didn't matter which—while the other had to be cold. And now he was explaining why he didn't serve veal in his restaurant. "The quality is inconsistent, and there's too much controversy over the way calves are raised. The veal I'm serving you today has been raised without cruelty—lovingly, in fact—by Pennsylvania farm kids who are given charge of the calves. They keep them in roomy stalls and feed them milk replacement. There may be more cruelty done to the kids who form a bond with the calves and then have to give them up for the market."

As noon approached, I sensed the pace of the telephone and restaurant deliveries picking up, though Deux Cheminées was closed to diners on Mondays. The béchamel sauce for the soup roiled in its kettle. "I'm going to play the piano," Blank said, placing three saute pans on flaming burners. "That's what line chefs say when they go into high gear." While butter melted in the pans, he placed the veal slices between sheets of waxed paper and flattened them with the side of a cleaver. Then he dusted them with flour. "With twenty-one slices and three pans, that means seven slices in each. I don't know if I can do it." He added a fourth skillet. The veal cooked quickly and was removed to a platter. Blank threw chopped shallots into the pans followed by a splash of Madeira that ignited spectacularly. When the flames subsided, he added beef stock, tomato paste, lemon juice, and mustard. Then, quick as a wink, twenty dinner plates were readied with veal, potato, quince, and snap peas (the formerly mysterious *mange-tout vapeur*). Each student carried a plate upstairs to a dining room where tables were set and the soupe aux choux-rave, made earlier by the Restaurant School students, awaited. I tried to eat slowly so that I would pay attention to individual flavors and the interaction of ingredients. But my plate was clean before I knew it. Someone uttered a South Philly phrase: "So good you want to die."

Blank joined us but did not eat. Someone asked if he had ever taken a cooking class. "Years ago," he said, "I was in a men's class taught by Julie Dannenbaum. Julie was one of the pioneers, a contemporary and friend of Julia Child. James Beard sometimes came to teach her classes, and so did Diana Kennedy, the authority on Mexican food. Julie also got Georges Perrier to teach. That was when Le Bec-Fin was a nine-table restaurant on Spruce Street. Does everyone know who Perrier is?"

Was he kidding? Chef Perrier was the city's most consequential French import since Joseph Bonaparte.

Blank was asked about the amount of cream and butter that he and Perrier used in making classic French dishes. "I am a culinary libertarian," he said. "I think everyone should form their own taste and orientation. The trouble most people have with food doesn't come from the ingredients but from their heads. We can always eat smaller portions, but who has the will power to do that? I don't. And it's hard for someone like me to get away from food. It always finds me. Before I went to Europe this summer, I was in Maine, where folks found out I was a chef and kept bringing me fresh salmon and other things to cook for them." He shrugged. "I can't say no."

3.

Turkey and Muskrat

WHEN I REPORTED to Deux Cheminées for the second lesson, the unexpected death of Pierre Franey was in the news. The chef and writer, whose column had appeared for many years in the *New York Times,* had suffered a heart attack while teaching a cooking class aboard the *Queen Elizabeth II.*

"I'll miss Pierre," Blank told our class as we assembled in the foyer. "He cooked in my kitchen at three Book and Cooks." Blank was referring to the Book and the Cook Fair, a yearly convergence of cookbook authors and local chefs in Philadelphia. "He invited me to cook with him at his house on Long Island. I'm very sorry I never found the time to go."

Down in the kitchen, Blank rapped on a copper sugar cooker to get our attention. "I'm going to start with *crème caramel.* This is one of my favorite desserts, along with *oeufs à la neige,* which is egg floating in *crème anglaise.* I'm sure you're also familiar with *crème brulée,* a 'burnt' custard that supposedly originated by accident in an English boarding school. Today's *crème caramel* is based on a Julia Child recipe to which I add Grand Marnier, ground dried orange rinds—a Provençal touch—and Assam tea. In my opinion, a pastry chef who can make crème caramel properly should get four stars, and one who can't should get minus stars. But people hiring chefs these days just look at their résumés. They don't make them demonstrate their cooking."

He began to crack eggs. "I have found, over the years, it's best to crack eggs on a flat surface. A sharp surface, such as the edge of a bowl, makes them fragment. Remember that eggs separate best when they're cold but should be beaten when they're warm. You can solve this by setting the bowl of separated yolks inside a bowl of warm tap water."

When the custard mixture was ready for the oven, Blank started to make risotto, removing the stems from portobello mushrooms and cutting the caps into wedges. "Do you know about portobellos? That's port-o-bell-o, by the way, not port-a-bell-a, as some call them. They're a marketing gimmick that a grower came up with when he let his criminis get too big and didn't know what to do with them. They're wonderful for soup and grilling, though the grill turns them black. I'll put the mushrooms in last, but I want to have them ready."

During a break I spoke with students who had taken Blank's courses before. This present group seemed less contentious than some others, they said. There had been friction in the past, particularly when vegetarians had attended. Those students certainly would have protested Blank's next demonstration. He stood at the island, long knife in hand and half a dozen live lobsters arrayed before him. "These are American lobsters, but the word *Américaine* in this classic recipe apparently has nothing to do with American cookery. It's just a quirk of French culinary nomenclature, like *sauce Espagnole*, which has nothing to do with Spain, and Hollandaise, which has nothing to do with the Netherlands. Some say the term should be "Amoricaine," which is a name that originated in Brittany. In any case, *lobster Américaine* is one of those dishes with peasant origins that has transcended class and is served in the best restaurants. Georges Perrier dictated the recipe to me. Of course, he said it's the only way to do the dish. Once lobsters were plentiful in America as far south as Pennsylvania and Delaware, but now Maine lobsters, so-called, often come from Nova Scotia. Be wary of soft-shelled lobsters in the summer months when they're sold, soft and mushy, to tourists."

With that he set a lobster apart from the others, placed the knife blade along the middle of its back, and swiftly bore down. After a few more strokes, the creature was in small twitching pieces—a more-merciful death, I reckoned, than dropping it in boiling water. Blank dispatched the other lobsters and sauteed them in olive oil and some of their juices. Then he made a conflagration with cognac, and when that reduced, he added fish stock, tomatoes, a *bouquet garni* with fennel seeds, and beef demi-glaze.

It was time to finish the risotto. To the onion sauteed in olive oil, Blank added rice, using a wooden bat to stir and coat, then poured in white wine. "For one cup of rice, add one cup wine," he said. "After it reduces, gradually stir in five cups of liquid. It can be chicken, vegetable, or fish stock, though not everyone likes risotto with fish stock." He reached into the bowl where eggshells had been discarded and put half a shell on the counter. "This is an old-fashioned way of keeping track of the amount of liquid stirred in, a half-shell for every ladle-full. You could also use toothpicks. There are lots of customs like this. There was a time, for instance, when cooks in monastery kitchens timed meat in the oven by the number of rosaries recited. To this day, it's considered bad form to whistle in kitchens because, long ago, that could have disrupted the recitation and skewed the timing."

When the risotto was ready, we headed up to the dining room. On the way, I stopped to look at a photograph of Blank standing between Pierre Franey and Louis Szathmary. Just to my right was the restaurant office where a man in cutoff jeans and a gray sweatshirt was taking phone reservations. He had short graying hair and a brisk, commanding manner. He saw me looking at the photograph. "Two down, one to go," he said. "I told Fritz he'd better watch himself crossing the street." It was the first time I'd heard Blank called anything but "Chef" in his restaurant. This was Neil Gorse, I would learn in time, one of Blank's closest friends.

Upstairs, the lobster, risotto, and *crème caramel* were served. Blank sat among us, without a plate. He waved his hand, as if directing musicians.

"Dive in, as my mother used to say."

The third and final class of the series fell on the Monday after Thanksgiving. Chef Blank had turkey on his mind. "My staff tells me I'm the turkey queen, even though we're not open on Thanksgiving. Deux Cheminées is not that kind of family restaurant. But I cook a holiday turkey for the employees, and they love it. Part of my secret is roasting at three-fifty. The food police might call for three-sixty to three-eighty, but that's too high. Also, most people don't know that uncooked turkey should be refrigerated at thirty-two degrees because it deteriorates easily. Since most refrigerators are kept at thirty-eight to forty, you should put a bag of ice inside the bird.

"I've had to suffer a lot of bad birds in my day. My mother overcooked the turkey every year. She constantly pestered my father: 'Do you think it's done? Do you think it's done?' But he didn't have a clue. For the last twenty-six years, I've had Thanksgiving with the same two-dozen friends, and for nearly all that time, the recipe changed every year. Then, four years ago, I found a recipe, first published by *Gourmet* in 1953, for something called Thompson's Turkey, and I've insisted they use it and not change it. I have clout because I'm the carver. The production is actually more fun than the eating. It involves shrouding the bird with cheesecloth—don't use aluminum foil; that steams the bird—and cooking for twelve minutes per pound, basting every twenty minutes with one-third stock, one-third clarified butter, and one-third brandy. It really works. Unfortunately, one of our group was caught in traffic this year, so the cooks tried to keep the turkey warm in the oven and ruined it. Did any of you have a Turkey Day calamity?"

The other man in the class raised his hand. "Yeah, this was a big deal for me, my first turkey. Most of my life I've been scared to death of cooking, but I decided to learn because my wife is an even-worse cook than I am. I was doing OK with the Thanksgiving meal until the kids turned the oven off by mistake."

"A capital offense," Blank said. "Well, you won't have to relive the trauma because you can see that turkey's not on our program today. The closest we come is chicken with spinach and truffle stuffing." He went into action, cutting and carving and splashing wine into a copper vat. He deboned a chicken and stuffed it with truffles that he said cost $38 a can. While discoursing on poaching and boiling meat (out of fashion in recent decades) and on black versus white pepper (the white has a mustier taste), he sewed up the bird with twine and a needle he called an *aiguilette,* then shrouded it in cheesecloth that had been dipped in basting solution. "I'm using the basting mixture I just mentioned for Thompson's Turkey: one-third each clarified butter, chicken stock, and cognac. The bird weighs four and a half pounds, which I multiply by twelve minutes per pound to get a cooking time of fifty-four minutes. Notice that I'm using vegetables in place of a rack in the roasting pan." He placed the chicken in the oven with several others made ready before class.

While the birds cooked, Blank kept us entertained by preparing and serving poached oysters with Hollandaise sauce. He also made rice pilaf by sauteing onions and mushrooms into which he stirred one part converted rice to two parts hot chicken stock. Eventually he pulled one of the chickens from the oven and pushed at it with his finger. "This is how I test for doneness," he said, holding up his left hand and making a loose fist. With his right index finger he pushed the fleshy part of his left hand between his thumb and forefinger. "If you make a relaxed fist, the flesh you push will feel soft. That's what 'rare' is like. Make a tighter fist and you can simulate 'medium.' With a tight fist, you have 'well done.' Try it at home; you'll find it works."

Just before we went upstairs to devour the chicken, Blank announced that anyone among us could spend a Thursday working in his kitchen. "You'll see me in a different way when I yell and scream," he said. "No, I'm kidding. I only grumble a little. There's no charge, but I'd expect you to make a donation to my favorite arts group. Georges Perrier would charge you a thousand dollars for the same thing and maybe scream at you as well."

Someone in the cooking class mentioned an all-you-can-eat muskrat dinner at the Lower Alloways Creek Fire and Rescue Company, near Salem in southern New Jersey. For the sake of culinary ethnography, Chef Blank said, he felt it was his duty to attend. Besides, his aunt had cooked muskrat years ago, and he wanted to try it again. I wangled an invitation to join him.

I met him at the restaurant on a cold and murky afternoon, entering by the delivery door on Camac Street. I did not follow the stairs down to the kitchen but turned right at the entry landing, climbed a few steps, and ventured through the serving pantry into a dining room that was in darkness except for a bit of pantry light that put an eerie glow on the tables set for dinner. Blank was waiting for me in the foyer, wearing checked chef's pants, a denim jacket, and a black sweatshirt that proclaimed "San Francisco" in big gold stitching.

We walked half a block to where the restaurant's car was garaged. It was a dove-gray sedan of ample dimensions for the chef. Behind the wheel, Blank seemed to have only a casual interest in the goings-on around us, directing the big car along Locust Street like a boatman easing a barge down a slow river. After a few blocks he stopped, well away from the curb, and got out to use a cash machine. When he returned he handed me a sheet of paper, neatly typed. "You're the navigator," he said, "study up." The paper was titled "Muskrat Dinner 6:00 PM Saturday." The directions that followed were in large, bold type for ease of reading in a car at night. Blank had included three numbers to call in the event we lost our way. A good chef leaves nothing to chance.

"So, who will mind the stoves tonight?" I asked, aware that he was playing hooky on a weekend night.

"The line cooks," he said, "but they always do. I never do turnouts, the actual cooking of orders. Earlier in the day I make sure all the prep work is done so that turnout runs smoothly, which means I often do a lot of the prep myself. All I do at dinnertime, when I'm there, is check the sauces. Or deal with spats and tantrums among the staff."

"Are those a problem?"

"Not really. If two employees have a falling out, I call them into the office and make them deal with it right away. But things are generally pretty harmonious. Nothing like the General Wayne Inn."

Blank was referring to a very old restaurant in Merion, west of the city, where a young chef who was also co-owner had been shot dead in the restaurant office. Weeks had passed, but the police had not produced a suspect.

"I knew the guy," Blank said. "He was a hard worker, a perfectionist. Trouble was, the dishes that were popular at his previous place didn't go over with the old-timers at the General Wayne. He and his partner, another chef, had to be losing money. Plus, the dead man had a furious temper. Those are some volatile elements."

"I read about it," I said. "I also read that a Hessian soldier haunts the wine cellar. He killed a colonial soldier, and the soldier's widow killed him. Another ghost supposedly hangs out in the bar and pinches women's bottoms."

"A randy old customer, just as likely."

"You don't believe in ghosts?"

"I prefer science to the supernatural."

"Is there any chance Deux Cheminées has a ghost?"

"I don't think so. But, speaking of spooks, there's evidence that Richard Nixon stayed there when it was the Princeton Club."

"What evidence?"

"Nixon was in the service, stationed at the Navy Yard. And once when we were renovating, we found a strange tangle of wires in the crawl space." Blank laughed.

At Washington Square, he took Seventh Street up to Race, then the Benjamin Franklin Bridge across the Delaware to New Jersey.

"We're close to Pennsauken, where I grew up," he said. "It was called 'Cattail City,' after the marsh vegetation. It's hard to imagine now. What used to be open meadows is all built over. Even ponds were filled in. Chandler's Run, a creek that ran into the Cooper River, is entirely underground, diverted into concrete culverts. Where Route 130 meets the old Marlton Pike and Kaigen Avenue, at Airport Circle, there really was an airport. The circle made a direct link to Ferry Avenue and the Camden-to-Philadelphia ferry lines. No more."

"When did your family get here?"

"My grandmother, Mary Catherine Blank, emigrated from southwest Germany in 1884. She was a farm girl, just fourteen. She married my grandfather straightaway, and they had nine children, eight boys and a girl. My father was the youngest. She became a widow the year I was born. When I was three, my father was in a terrible motorcycle accident, had a leg amputated, and was hospitalized for nearly two years. We had no medical insurance, so my mother worked two jobs. Weekdays she earned $4 an hour in the city, and on weekends she waitressed at a local pizza joint. She always made breakfast for my brother and me and packed us lunches on school days. At 5 p.m. we sat down together for a hot supper. In the years right after my dad's accident, the volunteer fire company collected groceries to give to us, but I don't think we ever felt embarrassed that we had less than our neighbors.

"My grandmother took care of me a lot of the time. I became the joy of her life, especially because I showed so much interest in her kitchen. Everyone in the neighborhood called her Mom Blank, and she often cooked for community events like weddings and fundraisers and picnics. She loved to do it. I was always in the middle of everything, watching and learning and helping. The other day I ran into an elderly cousin at a cooking demo, and we reminisced about our grandmother's food, especially her potato salad.

My cousin said it was too bad *Grossmutti's* recipes had been lost. I told her I could do all her dishes, including the potato salad. Maybe one day I'll do a Blank family meal at the restaurant."

"Did you speak English or German with your grandmother?"

"German. That wasn't unusual in our polyglot community. You heard German, Italian, Polish, Ukrainian, Yiddish, and a bit of Spanish. Most of us could say a little bit in all those languages: 'Hello,' 'See you later,' 'Nice day, isn't it?' 'Go fuck yourself.' My only problem was that I spoke English with a German accent. I had to lose that fast when I got to school. It's the usual story from that time. We were poor but didn't know it because we lived in a tight community. We had no municipal sewer, just cesspools and outhouses. In our own house, we had no running hot water until I was thirteen. The streets were unpaved, rutted. In winter we filled potholes with ash from our coal stoves. Still, the tinkers came through, along with the knife sharpeners and the hucksters. Cellars were full of preserved food. You saw chicken coops, duck pens, and rabbit hutches all over. Some neighbors kept geese, some had horses. One of my cousins raised turkeys that he killed and dressed every year for Thanksgiving. Imagine all that today in this sea of cars and roads."

"Were you always called Fritz?"

Blank laughed. "That's a bit of a secret. My given name is Frederick Carl Blank Jr. I was Fritz to my grandmother, but my mother nicknamed me Binky, after a company that made baby combs. So I was Binky Blank. I never gave it much thought until I left the neighborhood grammar school, which had a sixth-grade population of twelve, and went to a huge junior high. My new classmates thought 'Binky' was childish and hilarious. I felt scorned and outcast. So I became Fritz."

We were traveling south on Interstate 295 now, following the Delaware River. "Do you know about the caviar industry that was here years ago?" Blank asked. "There wasn't much demand for it locally, so it was exported, at great volume and profit, until the sturgeon were gone. Now there's talk that the fish is making a come-back in the river."

We continued downriver for about an hour, eventually passing through the old town of Salem, site of the first Quaker colony in North America. At last we came to the Lower Alloways Creek Fire and Rescue Company, in a one-story building beside a country road. Some old boys at the firehouse door looked us over. They seemed edgy until Blank opened his jacket and displayed his girth. "I'm a chef," he said, "can't you tell?" They laughed and motioned us to the ticket table. We paid $20 each for all the muskrat we could eat, plus fixin's, the proceeds to go to the fire company. A trophy case near the ticket table displayed a stuffed muskrat. The animal was rearing up on its hind legs, a posture that may show a horse to advantage but doesn't do much for a homely bog-dwelling rodent.

The dinner had drawn a crowd. Although it wasn't six o'clock yet, several shifts of muskrat eaters had already been served, and tables were being prepared for another sitting. We were directed to a communal table in a big, well-scrubbed room. The kitchen bustled with volunteer cooks, servers, and washers. Servers brought green beans, beets, coleslaw, and potato salad to our table along with paper cups of tomato juice spiked with horseradish. Then the muskrat arrived, cut into smallish pieces and heaped on a platter. The meat was the color of mud and, to me, had a muddy flavor as well. Blank said it tasted "somewhere between goose and snapping turtle."

A nearby couple from Wilmington, Delaware, said they were culinary adventurers. The past summer they had driven country roads in Poland, exploring the origins of Polish-American cooking. This got Blank going on the subject of pig's liver roasted in cider vinegar, a recipe he said he had learned from a Polish friend long ago. When he opened Deux Cheminées, he changed it to calves liver in raspberry vinegar—"raspberry vinegar was big then, in all the food magazines"—and put it on the menu as liver à la Polonaise.

"As it happened, Georges Perrier was given a similar dish by Paul Bocuse. 'Well,' I told Georges, 'Bocuse must have a Polish friend, too.'"

We took modest second helpings of muskrat, perhaps shamed by the news that a frail old man at another table had eaten so many portions his server lost count. For dessert we were given ice cream in Dixie Cups, with wooden spoons wrapped in paper—"The only way to eat from a Dixie Cup," Blank said, brandishing his spoon.

Two men at the end of our table said they were from Delran, New Jersey, about seven miles northeast of Blank's childhood home. "I used to work summers at Millside Farm in Delran," Blank told them. "Cows were milked at noon and midnight, sixteen hundred of them, and sometimes they had to be driven across Route 130, which divided the farm."

Soon Blank went to the kitchen to take some snapshots. He returned to tell us that eight hundred "rats" had been cooked, and that this was the sixtieth year of the muskrat dinners. Trappers delivered the animals skinned, he'd been told. At more than three bucks a pound, the meat was worth more than the pelts. First the animals were quartered and salted, then washed and frozen for two weeks. After defrosting, they were parboiled in pressure cookers, seventeen minutes for the rear quarters, fifteen for the fronts. Blank had asked a woman about the seasonings they used (bay leaves, he guessed), but she wouldn't tell him. "Whatever it is," he said, "I think I can improve on it." Next, the 'rats were deep fried in corn oil. The year before we went, the 'rats didn't thaw enough and turned out tough—a muskrat dinner disaster.

We drove back to Philadelphia accompanied by a container of muskrat for the Deux Cheminées staff. On the way Blank reminisced some more about his early days in New Jersey.

"You know, Campbell Soup was not far from us, in Camden. It's still there, of course. During the summers big trucks carrying tomatoes from the farms would careen down the rough streets, and sometimes lots of tomatoes would fall off. We had a kind of prearranged signal: When one of us heard the trucks and saw tomatoes in the road, we would bang on pots and everyone would come out and gather them up. Nothing better than a fresh Jersey tomato, even a bruised one.

"During high school I worked at the Crescent Pharmacy in Pennsauken, dispensing cokes. Another part-time worker there was a veterinarian who got me interested in animals. He told me about Delaware Valley College, an agricultural school up in Doylestown. My family was really very poor, and when I told my father I wanted to go there, he said I was on my own. Fortunately, the school had a work-study program, and they accepted me. I left home without a nickel. At college I waited tables, milked eighty cows twice a day, picked apples, mowed alfalfa, baled hay, and on and on. I took any job I saw posted on the bulletin board—trimming cows' hooves, inoculating chickens by the thousands, you name it. I got an occasional $5 bill from home, but otherwise I made it through four years on my own and got a bachelor of science degree. My finances improved a little when I went to the University of Maryland for graduate study in dairy science. I got teaching fellowships and other jobs that paid my way, including work at the USDA Agricultural Research Center while getting my master's degree."

After he fell silent for a while, I asked about his tattoos. I had noticed several of them on his arms, including a caduceus, emblem of the healing arts, and figured they might have something to do with his life before becoming a chef.

"I got them in San Francisco during my Army years," he said. "When I got my master's degree, the Vietnam War was really smoking, so I applied to the Army medical service corps and got a direct commission as a second lieutenant. A woman did the tattoos. She had a funny name, like Painless Polly. But she wasn't painless, even though I was drunk."

Dinner service was ending when we arrived back at the restaurant. Blank set out the leftover muskrat for his crew to try. Responses ranged from curiosity to amusement to disgust. There were no takers.

"Well," he said as he headed for his residence upstairs, "I guess I'll put my whites on and visit some tables. I don't think I'll tell them what I did today."

In the Chef's Classroom

*C*HEF BLANK shared his knowledge of food and cooking for the pleasure of it and not for the money, or so it appeared to me. His cut of our class fees, after expenses, probably didn't amount to much, and the demands of preparing and teaching on his days off seemed well beyond the call of his normal restaurant duties, which were rigorous enough. If that were not sufficient virtue for one chef, Blank also staged monthly lectures, or gastronomy seminars as he called them, on behalf of the American Institute of Wine and Food.

The AIWF was conceived in the 1970s by Jeremiah Tower, a civic-minded chef in California, as an educational program for schools. Julia Child and the winemaker Richard Groff later reshaped it into a membership organization for wine and food enthusiasts, amateur and professional. It functions nationwide through regional chapters run by volunteers.

The lectures Blank organized on behalf of the AIWF were held at the Restaurant School, in West Philadelphia, across the Schuylkill River from Deux Cheminées and not far from the University of Pennsylvania. The school occupied an Italianate-style mansion to which a utilitarian wing had been added. I drove there one fall evening to hear a beekeeper talk and was directed to a lecture room in the new wing that had cinder block walls and rows of desks bolted to the floor—a generic academic space but for the counter with a cook-top upfront and an angled mirror above it so students could see what was being done at the stove. The room was nearly empty and so quiet I could hear the hum of the fluorescent lights.

A lanky man stood at the cook-top counter, arranging containers of honey, honeycombs, and items presumably made of beeswax. He looked worried as he greeted me.

"Hi, I'm Tony Buzas."

A nom de plume? It seemed gauche to inquire. I asked instead, "So, how's the beekeeping business?"

"Not so good. I lost 75 percent of my bees last winter," a condition growing increasingly worse at that time in the late 1990s.

Just then Chef Blank walked in, wearing a denim jacket. A few others came in and took seats.

"How many are we?" Blank asked. "Seven? Jesus, I expected forty. Well, let me just say by way of introduction that I am Chef Fritz Blank, and for about three years now, I have been organizing these seminars on behalf of the AIWF to expand our awareness of the wonders of food. Tony Buzas's food, the honey his bees produce, is certainly wonderful because he doesn't cook it. Most commercial honey is cooked to keep it from crystallizing on the store shelf, and cooking takes away some of the flavor."

Buzas told us that commercial beekeeping in the United States got its start in Philadelphia in 1850 when a minister developed a hive with drop-in frames such as beekeepers use today. In his own business, Buzas said, he sold a small amount of pumpkin flower honey and spent most of his time transporting his bees up and down the East Coast to pollinate the fields of commercial growers.

"It's an essential service because pollination produces higher yields. Pumpkins, blackberries, melons, squash, and strawberries are some of the crops that bees can help significantly. The problem we're facing now is to maintain a sufficient bee population to do the work. Bees are vulnerable to a variety of environmental factors, and it would be a disaster on several levels if they dwindled to a point where they couldn't come back."

When Buzas concluded, we were invited forward to taste his bees' produce. The pumpkin flower honey was rich and complex, as Blank had indicated. When I put a bit of sticky honeycomb in my mouth, I had a sudden and unexpected memory of southern Virginia and the hives that my father's father had kept in his orchard. A child of ten or so, I would tag along with the beekeeper, Ivy Lewis, as he removed honey-laden frames from the hives. We wore gloves and hats with veils of mesh that tied around our necks. Ivy used a smoke-making device, shaped like a watering can, to sedate the bees. I liked Ivy, though he could be gruff. In private, when I was sure no one could hear me, I tried to speak in his mellow south Virginia drawl. So much memory from a morsel!

The following month, Blank's AIWF guest was Eileen Tait, the restaurant critic of the *Philadelphia Inquirer* who, after some thirty-five years, was nearing retirement. She wore a black dress and spoke fast. "I'm here because Fritz invited me and because Julia Child told me to be involved with the AIWF. I try to be accessible. Anyone can call me, a public relations person or even a chef. I happen to think PR people are important. Some of you might remember that soon after Craig Claiborne put Le Bec-Fin on the map, Mimi Sheraton, maybe out of spiteful feelings for Claiborne, called it one of the most overrated restaurants in the country. I felt bad for Georges and told him to get some PR advice. He did and it helped.

"I think I've learned how to get the best out of a restaurant by sizing up what dishes it's likely to do well. After so many years, I'm often recognized. I come into a place and suddenly everyone springs to life and spoils me. I'd prefer they not make a fuss. In fact, my idea of a great dinner is not a banquet staged by a food and wine society but something spontaneous, among friends. For my sixtieth birthday, we went to a crab shack. They didn't mess around. They left us alone. We ate our crabs, we drank our beer, we washed our hands in the sink, and went home. Speaking of home, I'd better be on my way."

"I appreciate Eileen," Blank said to me later. "She has a lot of power in this town but doesn't abuse it."

Soon I began driving Blank to some of his AIWF lectures. One December evening not long before Christmas, I picked him up outside the restaurant. He maneuvered himself into my van and grappled with the seat belt.

"Well, ho, ho, fucking ho," he said. "Are you in the Christmas spirit?"

"Not really. Are you?"

"Almost. I've got most of my Christmas cards in the mail."

"Do you send a lot?"

"Close to four hundred."

"Holy cow."

"Holy cow is right."

The AIWF speaker was Don Yoder, a member of the University of Pennsylvania faculty and an expert on Pennsylvania folkways.

"The subject is Christmas food traditions," he said, "which comes with a built-in problem. Which is older, the Christmas holiday or the food traditions associated with it? In the pre-Christian era, December 25 was considered the birthday of the Sun, a symbol of Mithras. Gloria Dei, or Old Swedes Church, on the Delaware waterfront, has the right idea with its procession of candles worn on heads and the fire department on hand.

"Santa Claus," he went on, "is the creation of the cartoonist Thomas Nast, who was German-born and therefore had a prototype in St. Nicholas, the patron saint of bakers."

Yoder read from the diaries of Elizabeth Drinker, a Philadelphia Quaker who, on Christmas of 1795, wrote "many attend religiously to this day, others spend it in riot and dissipation. We, as a people, make no more account of it than another day." (Egalitarian Quakers believed all days to be holy.) Then Yoder yielded the floor to food historian William Woys Weaver, who showed us an antique honey-cake mold from Holland and described baking springerle, anise-flavored Christmas cookies, using pewter molds made long ago in Philadelphia.

At the conclusion, Blank served Christmas cookies and cider.

"I spoke by phone today with my dear friend Micheline Edmunds," Blank said as I drove him home. "She was my first maître d'. As you probably know, Deux Cheminées started out in a smaller building, about a half-block south of where we are today. We opened on a shoestring, but fortunately Eileen Tait came right away and wrote a good review. So we were popular from the start. Micheline, who came from the south of France, was the ice cream on the pie. She had a telephone voice from God, though she couldn't say 'Spruce.' "I'd put an ad in the paper. She called and I heard this voice—'Aloo? This is Micheline'—and I knew I would hire her. She was perfect for the job. Some customers thought she and I were married. She eventually married Page Edmunds, who was an oil company executive. One winter night at the restaurant, when it was snowing outside, Micheline noticed that a man and woman eating at one of the window tables were looking kind of prissy-lipped, as if they had tasted something disagreeable. So she went over and asked if everything was OK. They didn't say anything, but the man frowned and pointed out the window. Under a streetlight two men were kissing in the falling snow.

"'Ah, oui,' she said with a big sigh. 'Soo romantic! Just like Pa-ree!'"

Like most organizations run by volunteers, the Philadelphia chapter of the AIWF had problems keeping its act together. Newsletters arrived late, sometimes promoting events that had already occurred. Some of the talks Blank scheduled had to be canceled for lack of public notice. He grumbled that the local AIWF organizers were inattentive and never came to his seminars. They had no interest in food science and history, he said; they just wanted to eat, and on the cheap. Still, Blank forged on with his program. One winter night the speaker was Gary Beauchamp, head of the Monell Chemical Senses Center, an independent research group informally connected to the University of Pennsylvania.

"Dr. Beauchamp represents one of the city's hidden treasures," Blank said. "The Monell Center is that place on West Market Street with the big sculpture of a nose out front. It calls itself—I'm reading here—'a nonprofit scientific institute dedicated to multi-disciplinary research on taste, smell, and chemical irritation.' There are many applications to food, obviously."

I could see why Blank and Beauchamp had hit it off. Beauchamp had a kind face and a contagious enthusiasm for science. His subject that night was salt—"one of the five principal flavors," he said, "along with sweet, sour, bitter, and umame, a Japanese term for the properties of MSG. At one time, salt was a heavily taxed commodity, and is the basis of the word 'salary.' These days, there is pressure on manufacturers, like Campbell Soup, to reduce or eliminate salt, but that's a tall order because salt is a cheap flavor enhancer. And tests suggest that it suppresses bitterness.

"Some animals love salt," Beauchamp said. "This includes guinea pigs, mice, cows, and deer. Others—cats and various other carnivores—do not, perhaps because meat and blood might be salty enough. As for humans, saltiness is a subjective matter, governed mostly by habit. If you have to reduce your use of salt, you can generally do so without feeling deprived. Your taste will adapt."

Out of Chef Blank's association with Gary Beauchamp and the Monell Center came a plan to demonstrate Monell's food-related findings to AIWF members around the country via traveling lectures. Blank agreed to host a pilot demonstration at Deux Cheminées. Nabobs of the Philadelphia food establishment attended as did several executives from AIWF headquarters in San Francisco.

"I hope we can pull it off," Blank told me several days before the event. "I've had a few tiffs on the phone with the San Francisco headquarters. They gave me the 'we-know-best' crap, and you know how I am about that."

On a Monday morning when the restaurant was closed and no cooking class was scheduled, I found Blank down in the pantry, carefully placing small red and green peppers in ramekins. We carried the containers upstairs and distributed them around a table set for thirty or so. Soon Marcie Pelchat arrived, the Monell Center staff member who would lead the demonstration. She arranged test vials and other paraphernalia at each place. Within a half-hour, the room was swarming with science-minded epicures.

"Hi, I'm Marcie Pelchat," she began. "Like most of you here, I'm interested in the connections between food and science. And like many, I'm a member of the AIWF and Les Dames d'Escoffier. I'm not sure I like the term 'foodie,' but I suppose that's what I am, especially when you consider that I named my daughter Madeleine, after Proust's famous pastry.

"Now, we all know what happens when you laugh while drinking milk," she said, pointing to a diagram of the human nasal cavity and tongue. "This demonstrates in the most elementary way that the nose and mouth are connected. But they're connected to an extent that many of us might not understand. Essentially, the sense of taste, which we associate with the mouth, only functions properly in conjunction with the sense of smell, an activity we identify with the nose. Let's see for ourselves. At every place, I've put three jellybeans of different flavors. First pinch your nostrils closed and then put one of the jellybeans in your mouth and chew it to see if you can determine a flavor."

I got no taste from my jellybean, only gummy texture.

"OK, now open your nostrils."

The flavor was immediately apparent: pineapple. We repeated the procedure with the two remaining jellybeans. The instant we let go of our noses, we got the rush of flavor: orange, then cinnamon.

Pelchat then had us test our flavor memories by sniffing the contents of four glass vials. To me the first sample smelled of bread. Blank said it made him think of an Asian market, though he couldn't pinpoint an ingredient. He was close; the flavor substance was basmati rice. I also missed identifying cayenne but got the remaining two: cumin and olive oil.

"The next test is for olfactory adaptation," Pelchat said. "Have you ever encountered a strong smell when you walked into a room but then after you stayed there a while, you no longer noticed it? That's what we call olfactory adaptation." I opened a vial that smelled of cinnamon and vanilla, then a second one that smelled entirely of cinnamon. When I sniffed the first bottle again, the cinnamon fragrance was much less discernible. "This is a technique that can be used to identify weaker flavor notes," she said.

Soon Pelchat gave us what she called a simple genetic test to identify those who might be "super-tasters," as she put it, as distinct from the unfortunates who would be labeled "non-tasters." "The genes in question here," she said, "haven't been identified by molecular biologists, but we know that in the Caucasian population, 70 percent are super-tasters and 30 percent are non-tasters. There are fewer non-tasters in other cultures, as in Japan where the non-taster population is just 10 percent. In terms of anatomy, the human tongue contains, on average, about five thousand taste buds, located in papillae, those bumps or ridges you can see with the naked eye. Super-tasters appear to have more taste buds than non-tasters do, and under the microscope, the taste buds of super-tasters look more organized than those of non-tasters. By the way, not all of our taste buds are on the tongue. A significant number are on the roof of the mouth and down the throat. Now, let's get on with the test."

There was a degree of competitive tension in the air as chefs, cookbook authors, restaurant critics, and other reputed *becs-fins* tasted a strip of paper impregnated with a substance I found so bitter that I recoiled and made a face.

"I saw some of you having the super-taster's characteristic reaction," Pelchat said. "Others had no visible response. Since this is a gathering of people seriously invested in food, I'm not going to embarrass the non-tasters by identifying them. It doesn't mean non-tasters should quit the food field and take up something else.

The degree of taste sensitivity varies within the categories of super-tasters and non-tasters and between genders. Women seem slightly more sensitive to flavor than men are."

After nibbling jellybeans and sniffing vials, we were pleased to be served a substantial plate of food from Chef Blank's kitchen, risotto cooked with white wine and truffles.

"We're having this dish because the truffles contain androstenone," Blank said. "That substance is also in celery and—don't let this spoil your appetite—human sweat. It's found in greatest concentrations in the saliva of male pigs. The smell of androstenone is subjective. Some will call it unpleasant—sweaty or urine-like—and others may call it woodsy or even pleasantly floral. And many, about 60 percent of adult males and 40 percent of adult females, can't smell it at all on first try but learn to pick it up after repeated exposure." Perhaps I wasn't such a super-taster after all. I liked Blank's risotto but was unable to identify any flavor from the truffles.

After the risotto we were served goat curry. This, we were told, was to test our reactions to unusual tastes. "People are usually less receptive to novel meat than to novel vegetables," Pelchat said. Maybe so, but I didn't notice anyone refusing their plate or pushing it away. I had eaten goat before, in London and in the Caribbean, even in Philadelphia, and I thought Blank's curry was delicious. I couldn't imagine disliking anything Chef Blank might cook.

Well, perhaps not *anything*. I knew that Blank, the erstwhile microbiologist, was curious about "delicacies" in various stages of rot. He had spoken to his cooking class about the affinity of some North American Inuits for fermented beaver tails. They would put the tails in a bag, he said, and keep them behind their wood stoves for about three weeks, a practice that sometimes ended in botulism poisoning. Now, following a course of cheese ("People like to eat things that smell bad," Pelchat declared) and salad dressed in *verjus,* to demonstrate how salt added to the liquid of unripe wine grapes reduces its bitterness, Blank took the floor to discuss his interest in "the processes of decay."

"I have degrees in dairy husbandry, dairy science, medical technology, and clinical microbiology," he began. "Before I became a chef, I was an analytical chemist at the U.S. Department of Agriculture's research center at Beltsville, Maryland. Then I accepted an Army commission and served five years as a clinical laboratory officer in the Medical Service Corps. When I left the military, I earned a master's degree in clinical microbiology at Thomas Jefferson University, just down the street from here, and was associate microbiologist at the Wilmington Medical Center. In the five years before I opened this restaurant, I was chief microbiologist at the Crozer-Chester medical and burn center. All this is not to toot my own horn but to explain why I'm so pleased by an event like this, which gives us a chance to talk about food from the standpoint of science. When I was at Beltsville, I got my first training in the science of taste. That was decades ago, so maybe you can understand my feeling that the wider dissemination of the kind of information we have heard today on the nature of taste has been a long time coming.

"Now, if you'll indulge me, I'm going to read from an article in *Granta*, the English literary magazine. It's called "First Catch Your Puffin," and it was written by Sean French, an English novelist who is attracted to foods that might repulse others because they look or smell disgusting, or because the food is not politically correct to eat, like whale meat, or because the creature seems too cute and cuddly to eat, like a puffin. French writes, 'I like blood. In Sweden you can buy a form of blood pudding in which the blood is mixed with meal and sugar. You fry it and eat it with lingonberry jam. The smell disgusts my wife so much she has to open all the windows when I cook it, but the children gobble it up because it's so sweet. I like parts of animals with improbable tastes and textures. The tang of urine in kidneys that attracted Leopold Bloom. The rubberiness of tripe which can taste like an underdone hot-water bottle. The blancmange consistency of veal's brain. Yes, veal. The ones transported live in lorries in front of which protesters throw themselves.'"

As I listened, I wondered if Blank was having a bit of sport with any food police who might be present, or with the AIWF dignitaries visiting from California. Well, he was entitled to have some fun. This was his restaurant, and he had just cooked and served a fine free lunch. He read on, "I've found very little that was actually beyond the boundary of the edible. One example was the Swedish dish *surströmming*. This is herring that is 'preserved' in salt water but has started to rot. You buy *surströmming* in cans that bulge slightly because of the continuing fermentation process. It is always prepared and served outdoors because, although it looks like normal herring, it smells quite startlingly of shit. Once, while staying in Sweden, I served it to some of my relations who had often spoken of the dish but never actually eaten it. Before opening the can, you have to bang a nail into it to release the pressure. I did so and was hit in the face by a miniature geyser of shit-smelling spray. After having a shower, I opened the can and served the fish in the traditional way, on a soft, thin bread with chopped red onion and sour cream. According to strict local tradition, we drank milk with it. Did it taste like shit? I don't know. I've never eaten shit. But shit certainly could taste like that. Having ingested a *surströmming* sandwich each, we all discovered an unexpected effect. The fermentation process continued in our stomachs, and we all began to burp uncontrollably. Having eaten shit, we were now farting through our mouths. Auden used to quote an Icelandic proverb which states that everybody likes the smell of their own farts. But then, wasn't it Larkin who said that sex was like having your nose blown by somebody else? This was like somebody else farting through your mouth."

As Blank read, I noticed some pained expressions in the group and tense smiles. When he finished, the meeting disbanded quickly. The Philadelphians returned to their offices, presumably, and the AIWF cadre headed for the airport and San Francisco. Several weeks later Blank told me that no one from AIWF headquarters had written to thank him for staging the event. In the months that followed, he held several more AIWF seminars at the Restaurant School and then called it quits. Attendance had dwindled almost to nil because of lax publicity by the institute. One evening, a lone woman came, a young Restaurant School student with her sights set on becoming a chef. She appeared less interested in the speaker's topic—trends in the food industry— than in what Blank might have to say about her intended profession. So he sent the speaker home, and for two hours patiently answered her questions.

Chef Eats Out

"*H*APPY NEW YEAR, and welcome to the Chinese Cultural Center. I'm your emcee, Donald, as in duck. We're celebrating the year 4695, the year of the ox. We're also celebrating the visit of our guest chefs, who have come all the way from Nanjing to prepare this very special ten-course banquet for you. If I may suggest to those of you who are unaccustomed to meals of this sort, don't serve yourself big Western-size portions, or you'll never finish. I'm sure you're all hungry, so let's get started."

Donald the emcee, exceedingly slender, seemed very hungry indeed. We needed no more urging from him to take from the communal platter just delivered to our table. Chef Blank led the way, manipulating his chopsticks as though they were his everyday utensils.

"I once tutored in an Asian household," he said. "I sometimes stayed for meals, and they taught me to use chopsticks. Chinese cuisine is my favorite. Some day I might take the cooking classes they hold here at the center."

The Chinese Cultural Center in Philadelphia's Chinatown, was built in the 1830s. Some of the materials—tiles and enameled woods—were obtained from the old country. An inventory of the city's architecture calls the three-and-a-half-story structure a "rare and outstanding example of the Peking Mandarin Style in the United States." Chinatown was about a ten-minute walk from Deux Cheminées, and Blank said he often went there to buy rice wine or a cleaver or to eat at the two or three restaurants he preferred among the scores doing business there.

There were ten diners at our table. Four, including Risa and me, had come with Blank. We didn't know the other five, one of whom was a woman, possibly drunk, who giggled throughout the meal. The other two in our party were Blank's friends Alice Cundy, an emergency room nurse before retirement, and her husband, Ken, formerly a professor of physics at Temple University.

"Finish what's on your plate," Ken told Alice as our second course was delivered with ceremonial gonging.

"But you complain about my weight," Alice said.

"Eat it anyway. We're paying for it, and the chefs might think you don't like it."

Blank had warned me about Ken. The man was a fussbudget, he said. Ken often visited the restaurant at lunchtime, fretting about this and that and snooping around Blank's desk. But Blank was loyal. He respected Cundy as a scientist. And friendship was friendship.

Risa and I were becoming Blank's friends, too. This was the second time I had eaten out with him, after the muskrat dinner in southern New Jersey, and it would be by no means the last. Risa enjoyed his company, as well. They liked to speak German together and reminisce about Vienna. The two once spent an eternity at table determining the location of a snack stand they both remembered in central Vienna, poring over a street map Blank drew from memory.

When Blank ate out by himself, he would sometimes report back to me because he knew of my interest in the restaurant scene. He phoned one morning: "I went to Bookbinder's on a whim last night for lobster. Sam Bookbinder knows me. I ordered a two-pounder, and when I split it open, some of the roe looked underdone. So they took it back and plunged it in the pot that still had all the yucky, musty steam from the first cooking, which penetrated the flesh. It tasted like a moldy book, but I ate it anyway."

"You're too kind."

"I'm not kind. I didn't want to piss off the cooks."

At the Chinese banquet, I helped myself to another course while Ken fidgeted, impatient for his turn.

I turned to Blank. "Did you see that Susanna Foo won a chef's award from the Beard Foundation?" Foo's restaurant, which bore her name, was one of the most popular in town. The Beard Foundation operated from the food writer's former house in Greenwich Village, apportioning honors to the food trade.

"She doesn't cook much," Blank said, "but I guess that doesn't matter to the Beard people. I knew Jim Beard. I liked his down-to-earth approach to food. But when he died, the foundation got caught up in glitz and became a marketing tool. I went to the award ceremony every year but the last two. The last straw for me was a concoction made by one of the chefs being honored. It was so bad that plates of it were parked all over the place, uneaten. I still have the tuxedos I wore to the awards in my closet, in increasing sizes. One year, I'd gotten so fat I couldn't button my vest, so I asked a woman friend there to cut it down the back."

"I'm feeling that way right now," Risa said, looking ruefully at the next steaming plate circling our way on the lazy Susan.

The Book and the Cook Fair provided another opportunity to eat out with Blank. At restaurants all over the city, chefs prepared meals in tandem with visiting cookbook writers. In theory, if not always in practice, the Philadelphia dining community flocked to collaborations between Georges Perrier and Jacques Pepin, or between Jean-Marie Lacroix of the Fountain at the Four Seasons Hotel and Charlie Palmer of Aureole in New York. In addition to Pierre Franey, a pioneer of haute cuisine in New York, Blank had hosted Paul Bocuse, the great exponent of *nouvelle cuisine,* and

André Soltner of Lutèce. ("Soltner was difficult," Blank said. "A nice man but too hidebound to adapt to an unfamiliar space.")

Some months after the Chinese banquet, Risa and I joined Blank at a Book and the Cook brunch featuring John Martin Taylor, of Charleston, South Carolina. Taylor, who was known in the food world as Hoppin' John, had just published *Fearless Frying* and was appearing as part of the Book and the Cook at Chef Michael McNally's London Grill. Word of Blank's presence went around soon after our arrival, and Hoppin' John appeared at our table, a slim man of the South wearing a white dress shirt and jeans.

"Every time I do one of these things," he said, "I'm reminded I could *never* cook in a restaurant. Being told what to do in the kitchen just to please customers' tastes would bring out the worst in me. People get too carried away over food. I was on a foodie trip through Apulia last year and people got *bent out of shape* over the smallest thing. I told them, 'It's only food, you nitwits; how serious can it be?'"

Soon Taylor and Blank were discussing the broad range of southern cuisine.

"It's a *big* region," Taylor said. "Even the coastal region, where I come from, is enormous, with food customs that change from place to place. For instance, Yankees think they can find barbecue everywhere in the South. No. Barbecue exists only where the Germans settled."

A waiter served us fried dill pickles. Blank tried one and grunted his approval.

"I discovered them at a roadside place outside Savannah," Taylor said. "They no longer serve them there—don't ask me why—but I've got the recipe in *Fearless Frying*."

On that day, fried dill pickles joined Blank's repertoire.

Not all excursions with Blank had happy endings. One day I sat in on a strawberry shortcake demonstration he gave at the Reading

Terminal Market. Along with Chinatown and the Italian Market on Ninth Street, the Reading Terminal is a principal food emporium in the city, comparable to the Pike Place Market in Seattle and San Francisco's Ferry Plaza Farmers Market. My trouble in such places, where rows of merchant stalls groan with food, is succumbing to overload and losing common sense about what to buy or eat. That day, after Blank's talk, I dropped my guard and let him buy me a big, greasy pork sandwich, with onions and hot peppers, on a hoagie roll. I wolfed it down, to my regret that night when my kidneys painfully rebelled.

I had a better result one evening when Blank and I set out to attend a lecture on food science, then discovered we had misplaced the address of the event.

"The hell with it," he said. "Let's go to Tacconelli's for pizza." Tacconelli's was favored among cognoscenti for its pizza dough, and feared for its grouchy servers.

"Fine," I said. "I've always wanted to go there. Where is it?"

Blank laughed. "Damn, I forget. Let's go to Tony Luke's."

We drove to South Philadelphia, the city's Little Italy, and parked near an overpass close by the Delaware River.

Blank said, "I take refuge down here sometimes when things get too intense at the restaurant." Some refuge. Tony Luke's seemed little more than a bunker of a kitchen with a carport attached, all very *far niente*. The "carport" was the dining room, if you chose to stay and eat. Stars embedded in the pavement saluted local heroes Frankie Avalon, Bobby Rydell, and Chubby Checker. Blank went to a portal in the bunker and ordered a pork sandwich with peppers. I had my pork sandwich with broccoli raab and "wet" with meat juice. It was terrific and caused no remorse in my gut.

"People in my business are stuck up about what they think of as primitive food," Blank said, brandishing the remains of his sandwich. "They have the idea that cooks who work without measuring implements—just a pinch of this and a handful of that—are somehow slapdash and unsophisticated. Not at all. They don't use measuring gear because they don't need it. My grandmother proved that to me. By taste and practice, they know the right amount exactly."

Restaurants were opening all the time in Philadelphia, and Blank was curious to try them. During a Book and the Cook Fair, he passed up two popular events, one featuring George Vongerichten ("I don't agree with his philosophy of cooking"), the other with Daniel Boulud ("too stuck up"), in favor of one at a new Italian restaurant on East Market Street. The honored chef-writer was Lidia Bastianich, whom Blank had met in England at the Oxford Symposium on Food and Cookery. But on the day of the event, she was detained at Felidia, her restaurant in New York, and was not involved in preparing our meal. *Porca miseria!* A "pecorino" entree had no discernible pecorino in it. Lobster was undercooked. The risotto had no taste. We grumbled to ourselves but hadn't the heart to complain when Lidia came to our table to say hello. She had just come from the train station, radiant and charming and apologizing for her tardiness. Did she know her occasion was in the weeds? She did not, we decided, and we didn't want to be the ones to tell her. Her new restaurant did not stay in business very long.

A visit by a chef of Blank's stature helped a new place gain local recognition. He was aware of this, and if word got back to him by the grapevine that owners were treating their employees unfairly, he would stay away. Stephen Starr was a restaurant impresario who had opened more than a dozen profitable establishments. He had, in fact, held his wedding at Deux Cheminées ("Huppa and all," Blank said). In the initial months of a Morocco-themed restaurant, Starr's chefs complained in Blank's hearing that they did not have the time and kitchen space to do proper work. Moreover, Starr had consulted at length with another chef, a friend of Blank's with extensive knowledge of Moroccan cuisine, but then did not pay her, she said afterward. "This is the raggedy-ass mentality that plagues the restaurant business," Blank said, and he resolved to stay away from Starr's establishments.

Curious as he was about new restaurants, Blank was always up for returning to an old favorite. His most frequent haunt was Tai Lake, up a few doors from the Chinese Cultural Center. In the congeries of Chinatown restaurants, Tai Lake was distinctive for its display of live fish and frogs in tanks by the front door. It was also exceptional, in Blank's mind, for the variety of its menu. This included eel, valued in China for taste and health-giving properties and popular with Tai Lake customers, American as well as Chinese, who could order it braised with roast pork or filleted and served in a crockery pot of boiling spicy sauce.

"A lot of American people order the eel," the manager, Sam Leung, said, "sometimes fifty pounds a week." Leung's eels were caught in the bay waters and tidal streams of southern New Jersey, notably Lower Alloways Creek, which Blank and I had visited to eat muskrat.

Risa and I went to Tai Lake one evening when Blank was entertaining Micheline Edmunds, his first maitre d', who was visiting with her husband, Page, and her young niece and nephew from the south of France. "Micheline is my dear friend," Blank said. "She and Page spend summers in New Brunswick, Canada, and I sometimes visit them." We did not order eel at Tai Lake that night (perhaps they were out of season) but shared a large platter of bright red shrimp. Blank's French guests, for all their likely *savoir vivre*, might have been nonplussed by the fare, but he and I ate with the gusto befitting a reunion.

I asked Blank one day about the Sansom Street Oyster House, a venerable establishment about five blocks from Deux Cheminées. A neighbor, Bernie Glassman, had recommended the place to Risa and me some time before. Blank said, "The owner, David Mink, is an old friend." Blank seemed to know every restaurateur in town, and was friends with most of them. "In another incarnation," he said, "Sansom Street Oyster House was a place called Kelly's, on Mole Street, started by David's grandfather back in 1901. David opened the Oyster House, I think, in the early '70s. Chef Louis Szathmary liked to go to there when he was in town. I suspect he had his eye on their oyster plates; they had a valuable collection. A chef named Howard Mitchum, who worked in New Orleans and then Provincetown, did the Book and the Cook there every year. Howard was deaf and also a drunk. At the Oyster House, he would autograph his cookbooks, communicate by notes, and drink two cans of beer, all at the same time. He was an example of a chef who worked to support his drinking. I remember he was popular in Provincetown, on Cape Cod. He got fired a lot, so he was always moving around, but you could tell where Howard was cooking by the line of people outside the restaurant. I once walked past a place where he was working and saw him through the kitchen window, drinking from two cans of beer, as usual. I came by again just a few minutes later, but no Howard. I stuck my head through the window and there he was, stretched out on the floor. Well, he lived the way he wanted to. I have some of his books, with funny inscriptions and drawings."

Risa and I went to the Oyster House with Blank on a Wednesday evening. He was waiting for us inside, holding Mitchum's cookbooks for Mink to sign. We were shown to a table near the kitchen, and I ordered a local beer called Yards Cast Conditioned Oyster Stout and a half-dozen oysters. Blank had cherrystone clams. Risa abstained from shellfish, fearing allergy. Blank was not in the best of spirits. "I had to fire my pastry chef," he said. "He had a booze and coke problem, and thought he was indispensable. But he wasn't as good at his job as he liked to think. He was sloppy. He worked too fast. His predecessor, who was more conscientious, would come in at two. This fellow would show up at four and just careen through the desserts."

A handsome man of about fifty walked up to our table. "This is David Mink," Blank said.

Mink looked at me. "Are you Craig La Ban?" An inside joke. La Ban, the *Inquirer's* new restaurant critic, worked incognito and had recently given the Oyster House a favorable rating—more favorable, perhaps, than Mink had expected.

"Yeah," I said, "I'm La Ban, but don't give me away. Just comp our meal tonight."

"Not a chance, Craig, but thanks for the review."

"Were you surprised?" Blank asked him.

"My wife was the most surprised of all," Mink said. "She's from New Orleans and the biggest critic of our food."

"So you're the third generation in the business?" I asked.

"No, I took this over from my grandfather. My father was a lawyer. Once when my father was up in Boston for a convention of the American Bar Association, he visited the Union Oyster House. He was a big hit with the women waiters who liked that he belonged to a bar association."

Our entrees arrived, shad for Risa, scallops for me, and, by special request, *bluefish meunière* for Blank. Risa and I discussed with Mink the passing of Bernie Glassman, our affable Mount Airy neighbor who ran a graphic design company in Center City. He had been one of Mink's regulars at lunch.

"What a shame," Risa said. "Bernie was a sweetheart."

"The staff loved him," Mink said. "He was diabetic, so he was supposed to be careful."

"Like me," Blank said.

"He had five sons," Mink said. "One of them has been back to the restaurant, but I haven't seen Vera yet." Vera was Bernie's widow.

Blank repeated his Howard Mitchum stories for Mink.

"I once suggested to Howard," Mink said, "that we do a certain recipe of his for the Book and the Cook dinner—sole cooked in buttermilk. 'Hell, no,' he said, 'where did you get the idea for that?' 'The recipe is in your book,' I said. 'Jesus,' he said, 'I must have been drunk.' Speaking of recipes, Rick Nichols has been asking about the Philly tradition of eating fried oysters and chicken salad together. Who might know about this?" (Nichols was the *Inquirer's* principal food columnist, and in my view, the best food writer in town.)

"Maybe Will Weaver," Blank said, meaning William Woys Weaver, the food historian. "I'm surprised it's not on your menu, next to the oyster club sandwich."

"Yeah," Mink said, "the oyster club sandwich and a Manhattan, another classic combo."

Talked turned to Horn & Hardart, the chain of automated restaurants started in Philadelphia in the 1880s. "Joe Horn was a stickler for quality control and tasted everything," Blank said. "He would have an enormous batch of spinach thrown out if he thought it was gritty."

"For a time they served oysters," Mink said. "In the '40s you could get seven of them, sauteed in butter, for forty-five cents."

"And fresh coffee for a nickel," Blank added.

Over dessert—rice pudding for Blank, apple brown Betty for Risa and me—Blank spoke of some carved souvenirs he'd bought on a recent trip. "As if I need them," he sighed. "I may be crazy for buying so much, but the knickknacks mean something to me. I'm a nester."

Several days later, while shoveling snow from the driveway we shared with the Glassman house, I saw Vera and told her of our dinner at the Oyster House.

"Bernie often had lunch there," she said.

"I know. David Mink said they really miss him."

"It's funny. You eat at a restaurant long enough and it becomes like another home. As a diabetic, Bernie had to watch the sweets. One of the older waitresses, who knew him well, wouldn't serve him dessert."

Fritz, George, and Georges

ONCE DURING A BREAK in our classes, Chef Blank saw me looking at the books he kept on a shelf in his staff dining room. They included *The Joy of Cooking*, Craig Claiborne's *New York Times Cookbook*, and both volumes of *Mastering the Art of French Cooking*, all in protective bindings.

"I have these here mostly for the apprentices," he said. "A good way to test a recipe is to give them one from these books and see how they fuck it up. Usually they don't read carefully or else they don't understand what's written and try to cover up by improvising. I have more books upstairs, you know. Have a look if you like."

I'd already had a look at the library but didn't tell him so because I wanted to see it again. Two floors above the basement kitchen, in a room nearly half a city block in length, Blank kept more than twelve thousand publications relating to food: cookbooks, histories, dissertations, memoirs, pamphlets, periodicals, menus, travelogues, and on and on. I'd heard him say that he owned more books by and about James Beard than the Beard Foundation in New York. Diners were routinely invited upstairs for a peek at the library, and after our first meal at the restaurant, the affable captain, Carlo Cicchini, had escorted Risa and me upstairs.

"Do you use cookbooks?" Carlo had asked.

"Only as a last resort," Risa said.

In addition to allowing his customers a peek, Blank also made his library available to food historians, journalists, cookbook writers, and the occasional home cook like me. I returned to Deux Cheminées a few days after he had extended his invitation and found him on the kitchen phone, unsnarling a botched order. He was plainly annoyed at the offending purveyor but kept his temper and ended the call politely. He led me up two flights of stairs, then dropped into a chair to catch his breath.

"As culinary collections go," he said, "mine isn't especially large, believe it or not. And it's not particularly old, like Anne Willan's, or particularly focused, like Will Weaver's is on Pennsylvania food lore. But it does reflect my personal interests, all revolving around gastronomy."

A voice on the intercom summoned Blank back down to the kitchen. As he left he handed me a piece of paper. "The list is incomplete," he said, "but it will give you an idea." Indeed, his list made clear the culinary and academic range of Blank's collection. I read: "Agriculture, Aquaculture, Archival Menus and Other Food-Related Ephemera, Cookery, Ecology, Evolution of Gastronomy, Food Art, Food-Borne Diseases, Food History, Food Marketing, Food and Holidays, Food and Religion, Food and War, Foodways and Culture, Food Technology and Science, Hospitality Business, Physiology and Psychology of Taste, Wine and Drink."

I looked around. Books were everywhere, in ordered ranks and files. Much of the shelving was fashioned from planks resting on empty quart cans of College Inn chicken broth. On the highest shelves were souvenirs of Blank's travels: mugs, condiment jars, airplane liquor bottles, mineral water bottles, wine bottles, soda water cans, the tidy trophies (some might say the detritus) of a collector and homebody. Six of the wine bottles were from Mouton Rothschild, the Bordeaux estate that commissioned eminent artists to design each year's label. Of these, I recognized the 1973 label by Saul Steinberg and one by Keith Haring for the 1988 vintage.

On a wall near the entry hung an award from Delaware Valley College, the farm school that Blank had attended, presented to

Distinguished Alumnus Fritz Blank, class of 1964. Beside that was a certificate from the Washington Square West District Association for Blank's "contributions to the quality of life" in the neighborhood. And next to that was a large poster of an enormous chef. It was inscribed, "To my good friend and colleague Fritz Blank" and signed "Chef Louis Szathmary (have knife, will travel)."

I nearly overlooked a framed photo of a slender man with wavy black hair. He was wearing chef's whites and reading a cookbook by Arthur Gold and Robert Fizdale, the pianists and men-about-New York who wrote about food for *Vogue*. The thin fellow was Blank, in a day when he sported a mustache but no beard.

On a shelf to my left, I saw *The English Housekeeper, Lady's Assistant*, 1801 and a set of cookbooks published by the Campbell Soup Company. Farther on I came to a row of M.F.K. Fisher's works, several literary anthologies on food, and Raymond Sokolov's *Why We Eat What We Eat*. Along the wall to my right, near some whimsical cow-themed mementos and *The Illustrated Encyclopedia of Metal Lunch Boxes*, were some four-dozen books on Austrian cooking, as well as volumes on other ethnic cuisines: Native American, Albanian, Bulgarian, Greek. The collected correspondence of the eighteenth-century botanist John Bartram shared a shelf with *Marijuana Botany: The Propagation and Breeding of Domestic Cannabis.*

While inspecting another row of titles, I was startled by a pair of staring eyes. I'd awakened Blank's cat from her nap on an open stretch of bookshelf. Some days before, the cat had come downstairs to survey the cooking class assembling in the foyer. She had circled the room diffidently and then, clearly unimpressed, returned upstairs with the studied disdain of a maître d'.

I progressed along the west wall of Blank's library until I came to a big CD player and several hundred recordings in neat arrangements: symphonies, operas, chamber music, and a cassette labeled "Chicken Dance." Further on, I arrived at a window where winter sunlight poured through with the vigor of spring. In front of the window, Blank had made himself a sylvan glade with potted plants and little mechanical fountains. His desk was nearby, and behind it was a television and a big leather-covered lounge chair, a cozy refuge for a tired chef. On the floor beside the chair were several books and a half-eaten bag of potato chips. The books included John Boswell's *Christianity, Social Tolerance, and Homosexuality* and Bill Bryson's *Made in America.*

Blank returned from the kitchen. He had been rearranging the library over the winter, he told me. "I can only do it little by little; otherwise I'll go mad. It reminds me of when I worked on the dairy farm. I milked cows at 5 a.m. and 5 p.m. and did the breeding and all that stuff. In the summer we cut and baled hay, tens of thousands of bales of it. We'd bring in a load, and a farm hand named Harvey Huntzberger would put it away in the barn, one bale at a time. God, Harvey was slow. But at the end of the day, he'd have them all in place. So my system in the library is like Harvey's, one book at a time."

There was more to the library than the enormous main room. Blank led me across the stair landing to a wood-paneled den that looked out on Locust Street. He kept his French, German, and Italian cookbooks here, he said, and the restaurant sometimes used the room for private parties. Next we took the stairs to the third floor, where he stored his periodicals. There were dozens of titles, some going back many years. They ranged from the popular (*Gourmet, Saveur, Cook's Illustrated,* etc.) to the outré. Among the publications unfamiliar to me were *Petits Propos Culinaires* and a newsletter called *The Curmudgeon's Home Companion.*

We returned to the second floor but instead of turning left to re-enter the library, headed straight, into the parlor of Blank's living quarters. He was quite right when he called himself a "nester." If the library didn't give enough evidence of his acquisitive tendencies, we were now in a sanctum where his nesting-ness was everywhere on display. The parlor, which didn't appear to be much used, was furnished, like the foyer downstairs, with smartly scavenged antiques.

"My bedroom is this way," Blank said. He led me down a narrow corridor past a galley-sized kitchen. The kitchen shelves displayed a collection of eggcups.

"Do you cook here?"

"Not much. I have a proper galley behind the library."

We walked past shelves of ceramic cows and a cuckoo clock, then entered a very big room, as bedrooms go, with a high ceiling, a fireplace with a carved mantle, and, opposite the mantle, a double bed with a curved Victorian headboard. I was not surprised to see neat stacks of books and magazines around the room. I noticed John McPhee's *The Founding Fish*, Maggie Paley's *The Penis*, Jeffrey Steingarten's *It Must Have Been Something I Ate*, and a pamphlet titled *Domestic Animal Bells From Around the World*. Paintings and prints of dairy cows covered the walls.

I said, "This may sound odd, but I can think of only one other man who had as much stuff as you do and kept his bedroom so tidy."

"You call this tidy?"

"I do. When is your birthday?"

"August 25. You're going to say it's a Virgo thing."

"Well, I suppose I could."

"So, who's the other neatnik?"

"My Uncle George. I used to stare into his closets. Nothing was ever out of place.

"A Virgo?"

"In fact, he was. August 23."

"I'll bet he wasn't a pack rat like me."

"You're probably right."

We went back to the library and sat at the big round table near the door. The tabletop had been fashioned from the restaurant's cast-off wine crates. Louis Szathmary smiled at us from his poster on the wall.

"I do miss Chef Louis," Blank said, "He was the collector's collector. Before he died he donated several hundred thousand items to the Johnson and Wales archives, in Rhode Island. He was amazing. He had a degree in journalism, a Ph.D. in psychology, and wrote for Chicago newspapers and most of the major American food magazines. Even though he didn't leave Hungary until he was in his 30s, his English was good. The language did trip him up now and then. He called me once to ask about a woman promoter in Philadelphia who had been pestering him to do something or other. He said to me, 'Freetz, who eez this woman?' I told him she's just a local publicist, a nice person, even if she's a little too aggressive now and then. 'She's a bulldozer,' is how I put it. That made Louis indignant. 'Bulldozer!' he said. 'Freetz, please, it make no difference to me if she's a lesbian!"

I asked Blank about his music collection.

"I've always liked vocal music, especially choral works. I'm sure you've heard of the Philadelphia Singers."

Indeed I had. They were one of the most accomplished choral groups in the nation.

"I'm on their board of directors. Every year I host a fundraiser for them in the restaurant. I recreate a meal from the time and place of an eminent composer. I cook the food that, say, Beethoven or Mozart or Rossini would have eaten, and members of the Singers perform the composer's music. I use the books in this room for reference and get more help, when I need it, from historians at Penn and elsewhere. History on a plate, you could say."

"Who are you doing next?"

"George Gershwin. He's not one of the classical pantheon, obviously, but *Rhapsody in Blue* is probably the best-known symphonic work by an American. Then there's his opera, *Porgy and Bess*, and all those great musicals, 'Strike Up the Band,' 'Of Thee I Sing. . . .'"

"'Lady Be Good.'"

"Yes, 'Lady Be Good,' 'Girl Crazy.' He had so many successes in a short life. I think he was thirty-eight when he died. But he lived well. His parents were Russian immigrants and they gave him a *feinschmecker.*"

"So what's the menu going to be?"

"I'm working on it. Why don't you come to the dinner and find out?"

Risa and I attended the Gershwin dinner with our friends Maysie and Tatnall Starr. We sat in the Gold Room, a clubby chamber with mahogany wainscoting and leaded glass windows. The menu, like Gershwin's music, seemed appropriate for many tastes. It began with martinis and roasted peanuts then proceeded to fish consommé with smoked whitefish dumplings to *coulibiac,* the classic French rendition of salmon served in pastry. After pausing for tea seasoned with cassis, we went on for five more courses, including corned beef with slow-cooked "slushy" cabbage and ending with *oeufs à la neige,* then coffee and crisp almond-flavored *mandelbrot.* Clearly, Blank was a culinary democrat, taking equal care and pleasure in replicating traditional dishes regardless of their rank in the culinary caste system.

While we ate, he toured the tables to explain his menu and provide some history. *Coulibiac,* he said, is associated with Antonin Carême, who cooked for Czar Alexander II in the prerestaurant years when chefs were privately employed. Gershwin's parents had emigrated from Russia and served *coulibiac* on special occasions. A more-common dish for him ("He ate it every day") was our fifth course, *tartarbrot,* raw sirloin sliced thin and served with sweet onions, cornichons, and black bread. And *oeufs à la neige,* eggs coated with hard-crack caramel, poached in milk and floated in *crème anglaise,* had been another favorite of the Gershwins. Blank told us: "A bunch of hotshots, like James Beard, Julia Child, Pierre Franey, and Jacques Pepin, were once asked what dessert they would want in a hypothetical last meal. They all said *oeufs à la neige.*"

Between courses an ensemble of the Philadelphia Singers entered the Gold Room and serenaded us with "I Got Plenty of Nothin'" and " 'Swonderful." Then came "Someone to Watch Over

Me." At that Risa and Maysie cried while Tat and I stared solemnly at the tablecloth. When the last crumb had been eaten or scooped away, Blank visited our table looking happy and tired. He discovered that Maysie knew the family of Peter von Starck, the late proprietor of La Panetière, the Philadelphia restaurant where Georges Perrier had gotten his start in America. In fact, the chairs we were sitting on, Louis XV in style and upholstered in striped silk, had come from La Panetière. "After Peter died and the restaurant closed," Blank said, "we got dozens of these chairs at auction. An appraiser told us that replacing the chairs today would cost seventeen hundred dollars each."

"Do you cook?" Blank asked Maysie.

"Not as often as I used to," she said. "But I got a good start. During a college year in Europe, I attended Le Cordon Bleu in Poitiers."

"I can top that," Tat said. "My grandmother sent her cook to train at Le Cordon Bleu in Paris."

"I suppose that shows how cooking has come up in the world, class-wise," Blank said. "We chefs were once considered servants, but we've been elevated lately. Who knows where it will end? I remember watching Georges Perrier once as he made a sauce. You know, he considers himself the best saucier in the world. Anyway, he performed his usual theatrics, and when he finished, he stood back to admire his work and declared, 'Here, made by God!'"

"Oopen ze windows! Ouvrez, ouvrez!"

Smoke assailed us from the front of the classroom where Georges Perrier was making *poularde farci*, capon stuffed with mushrooms and chestnuts. About forty of us watched this incendiary performance, the climax of three demonstration classes the chef was giving to promote his new cookbook, *Le Bec-Fin Recipes*. In the manner of Napoleon, whom he idolized, Perrier had marched us through a score of recipes, from *pommes boulangere, beignets d'huitres* and *poisson en papiotte* to the smoking *farci*. To me and perhaps to others in the room, it seemed that he had been building to this moment, rushing around the demonstration kitchen, barking orders, and brandishing a hand blender, like Punch with his cudgel. He also put me in mind of Vatel, the seventeenth-century chef and impresario who, in the service of Fouquet and the prince of Condé, brought his banquets to a climax with fireworks. As fretful assistants scurried to throw windows open, Perrier appeared neither alarmed nor contrite but in his element, amused and comfortable.

The Perrier classes were a supplement to the more-measured and low-key instruction I was getting from Chef Blank, Perrier's confrère and occasional student many years before. I signed on because Perrier seldom gave classes ("I am sooo bee-zeee") and because he was a phenomenon of the city, a chef of prodigious talent who, after more than twenty-five years as the proprietor of one of the best French restaurants in America, was still at the top of his game. And, I confess, there was another reason. For all his skill and scholarship, Blank was a German-American boy from New Jersey and not, like Perrier, an off-the-airplane Frenchman. Did Perrier's patrimony, I wondered, make him the better custodian of French culinary tradition?

Perrier's first home had been in Aix les Bains, near Lyon, where his mother cooked *choucroute* and *civet de lièvre* and made salad with greens that Georges, so he has said, helped her gather in the family garden. In the 1950s, the years when I was subsisting on boarding school s.o.s. and Blank was pulling sodas in Pennsauken, Perrier apprenticed himself to a casino hotel near Lyon, working seventeen-hour days and making his first *pommes de terre à la crème*. From there he went to the three-star l'Oustau de Beaumanière in Provence, then on to La Pyramide, the culinary temple of the great Fernand Point, where he became *chef poissonier*. All this before Perrier was lured to Philadelphia to cook at Peter von Starck's La Panetière.

It was good for Perrier that he made Philadelphia his home and not New York or Washington, as had his countrymen Pierre Franey, Jacques Pépin, Jean-Louis Palladin, René Verdon, and Alain Sailhac. In those early days, Perrier was shy, not the confidant showman he would become. Working in a city that had few celebrities outside of Grace Kelly, Marian Anderson, and Fabian, he had a better chance to stand out from the crowd. When his volcanic temper became known, when he began to throw plates in the kitchen, cuff underlings, and punch tradesmen (who sometimes punched back), Philadelphians were inclined to forgive. They were grateful to have someone of his accomplishment in town and took his irascibility to be a mark of authentic French-ness, perhaps of genius, even as they struggled in vain to correctly say "Bec-Fin."

For myself, Perrier's volatile temperament brought back old memories of a family vacation at a dude ranch in Jackson Hole, Wyoming. The chef there, a huge German named Otto, was said to make the best tomato aspic in the Rocky Mountains. Unfortunately, Otto became lonely and homesick in the remote environs of Jackson Hole. He drank a lot, and when he was drunk, he roared and rampaged and brandished the kitchen cutlery, terrifying his staff. The dudes rusticating there were enthusiastic drinkers themselves, but Otto's behavior was just too much. On a cloudless August afternoon in the majestic Tetons, beefy orderlies arrived in a black Mariah, wrestled Otto into a straitjacket, and carted him away as he sobbed and raged in his restraints. Watching the sad tableau, I was struck by how the chef's whites Otto was wearing seemed all of a piece with his straitjacket. From that day on, I was always alert to a possible linkage between excitable chefs and dangerous lunatics.

Still, I could admire Perrier from a safe distance. After all, he was revered for restoring the glories of French cooking to his adopted city. At the end of the eighteenth century, when Philadelphia was the world's boomtown and French cooks displaced from elsewhere manned its kitchens, gastronomes like Thomas Jefferson ranked the city second only to Paris. No one would presume to claim that today, but Perrier, more than any other chef or restaurateur, was the engine of Philadelphia's restaurant revival.

Around the time I attended his demonstrations, Chef Blank invited me to sit in on a class he taught at the Restaurant School on classic French cuisine. We met in a room nearly identical to the one used for Blank's AIWF lectures—windowless and empty of everything but bolted-down seats with swivel arms and a cook-top down front with an overhead mirror. But this time there was an audience of twenty or more student chefs. Most of them seemed of college age, a few clearly older who were changing careers. All wore white jackets and gray checked pants and looked tired, though they did their best to pay attention. Blank was worth hearing, a hands-on chef and restaurant owner who'd been called "a national treasure" by the Zagat Survey.

As he was inclined to do, Blank rambled at first, circling around his subject. He spoke of Antonin Carême, the "chef of kings and the king of chefs," who predated Escoffier and is credited with developing the simplified but refined style of cooking called *haute cuisine*. Yet not everything we think of as haute cuisine is French by origin, Blank said. *Coulibiac*, for example, the delectable salmon pie, came out of Russia, and Vichyssoise, the summertime soup of leeks and potatoes, originated in New York. Then Blank veered into a description of a vegetarian movement of the nineteenth century that began in Philadelphia and ended up in Battle Creek, Michigan. The breakfast cereal known as Post Grape-Nuts, he said, came from that era, the byproduct of a failed attempt to create a coffee substitute. The audience tried gamely to follow Blank's train of thought. Perhaps sensing their muddle, he got down to business.

"I have been a chef for more than twenty years and a cook for fifty-five," he said. "The last thing you want to listen to is some old fat French chef telling you how to cook classic cuisine. But I teach this class every semester to help you understand where most of the things you're learning to cook come from. So, let me ask, when you hear me say 'classic French food,' what associations do you have?"

The students were quiet for a moment, then a few mumbled "heavy" and "rich."

"I thought so. Now let me ask you, does Georges Perrier cook heavy, rich food?"

The response was unanimous: No, he did not.

"You're right. Perrier's food is delicious, balanced, not heavy or rich. But let me tell you something. He likes to say he has lightened up on his ingredients. But take his *beurre blanc.* The recipe in his new cookbook is the same one he's been using for twenty years. I know because twenty years ago, he gave me that recipe. My point is that classic French cooking is not about rich, heavy ingredients; it's about balance. No one flavor should predominate. All tastes should be subtle. That requires discipline, the discipline of knowing how a dish is put together, without gratuitous improvising, and how it is supposed to taste. Then you have to be able to make it consistently, time after time. You all have copies of *Larousse Gastronomique?* You will find there are two hundred and eighty-three egg dishes, listed by name. That doesn't include some ninety omelets. They are wonderful recipes but by no means easy. A fried egg, for example, is the most difficult thing to do correctly."

Before the class ended, Blank prepared *filet de boeuf Richelieu* (beef with a vegetable garnish), explained flambé, and showed the proper way to peel a tomato ("I learned this from Marcella Hazan") and flute a mushroom.

"Be careful that what you do is honest, genuine cuisine," he said in conclusion. "Don't make a mishmash by trying to reinvent the wheel. Then you'll be successful. Any questions?"

There were no questions.

Les Dames de Fritz

*B*LANK, I NOTICED, was affectionate and generous to women and they reciprocated, often greeting him with kisses. On social occasions, in the restaurant and elsewhere, it was not unusual to find him trundling happily through a crowd with lipstick marks on his cheeks. Some women, Risa among them, thought he was handsome. One woman admirer from New York even tried to court him, to Blank's amusement and mild distress.

He listened attentively to women and gave them credit when it was due. For example, he often praised Julie Dannenbaum, whose cooking classes he had attended before opening his restaurant. Dannenbaum was well known in the city and beyond. In 1964 she started what became the largest school for home cooks in the country. Her cookbooks, written in the 1970s and '80s, were widely read. ("They're wonderful, some of my favorites," Blank said.) She taught in Europe as well as Philadelphia, and she knew everyone who was anyone in the culinary galaxy of her time, including Julia and Paul Child, Simone Beck, James Beard, and Richard Olney, the expatriate cook, artist, and writer based in Provence. In his memoir, Olney recalled a profitable gig at Dannenbaum's cooking school in 1974. "In Philadelphia," he wrote, "classes—morning demonstration only—began the first Monday in December and ran through the week. The classroom was a small auditorium, a stage at front with counter-top, burners, and an overhead mirror, stoves and ovens behind. Julie was determined that I was going to make money on these classes; she was registrar and assistant. I never knew how many students were registered—fifty or more, at a guess.

That week paid for all my expenses during the seven months I spent in the United States."

One hot summer day, at Blank's suggestion, we met Julie Dannenbaum for lunch at a French restaurant not far from Deux Cheminées. Cool and composed in a gray checked suit, she was the most elegant diner in the room, but elegant without airs.

"I was a Pennsylvania farm girl," she said. "Granddaughter of a chef on the German Line. I studied at Penn State—home economics, it was called then—and later at Le Cordon Bleu in Paris. But my mentor was Dione Lucas."

I knew of Lucas, the first female graduate of Le Cordon Bleu and the first woman to host a cooking show on American television. "To the Queen's Taste" was broadcast on CBS in the late 1940s from Lucas's restaurant, the Egg Basket, on Manhattan's East Side. I never saw the show, but I passed by the Egg Basket many times, wishing I could afford to eat there.

"When I was a young mother," Dannenbaum said, "I watched Dione on a TV set with a tiny screen, praying the baby wouldn't fuss and distract me. I eventually took lessons from her in New York, catching a train at seven in the morning. In class Dione would dictate recipes while she was prepping. She had hands of gold. She became a very good friend. When the train arrived back in Philadelphia, I always got off carrying food. All the other women were carrying shopping bags from Saks."

I thought about the expression "hands of gold." I had heard Blank praise an apprentice for having "good hands," and I had sometimes marveled at his own dexterity when preparing food. But I found the concept unsettling. Could good hands be a gift bestowed on some at birth and denied to others—like me, perhaps? I put this to Julie Dannenbaum.

"Good hands come with good technique," she said. "The teacher has to demonstrate it, again and again. That's why watching a good cook is so valuable. If the student pays close attention, I think it's possible to learn by example."

"That certainly helped *me*," Blank said. "I watched my grandmother and I watched you. You always demonstrated clearly how to do things, and you showed us how to be comfortable handling equipment and ingredients. That gave us confidence, as well as a standard to follow."

"Well, I enjoyed teaching," Dannenbaum said, "even though the school was a lot of work and full of surprises. When my books were becoming successful, the phone started ringing off the hook. One day I answered and someone said, 'Hello. This is Craig Claiborne.' I said, 'Yeah, and this is Queen Elizabeth.' He said, 'I want to come to your school.' I said, 'Sure you do.' It was quite a change from being a cooking class student myself, commuting to New York by train. But it shows that hard work pays off."

In company with Julia Child, Nika Hazelton, and M.F.K. Fisher, Julie Dannenbaum was among the first to be named a Grande Dame of the international culinary society Les Dames d'Escoffier. She long remained active in the Philadelphia chapter, supporting programs to help women succeed in the hospitality industry.

Betty Groff was another of Blank's friends who could call herself a Pennsylvania farm girl. But unlike Julie Dannenbaum, she remained where she was raised, in the Amish and Mennonite farmlands of Lancaster County, close by the Susquehanna River and some ninety miles west of Philadelphia.

"My mother's maiden name was Groff," Blank told me. "I met Betty after I wrote to tell her that. We've been friends ever since." One spring day he announced he would be driving to Lancaster County to visit her, and invited me to join him. She would be taping a cooking show in her home kitchen, he said, and could use some help.

We drove first to Groff's Farm Golf Club and Restaurant, near Mount Joy, the principal family enterprise and a well-known destination in the Pennsylvania Dutch country. Betty's husband, Abe

Groff, met us beside the golf course. He was dressed for golf, but I could picture him as well in overalls and a gimme hat.

"The seventeenth hole here is a par four," Abe said. "You have to play it carefully because it has four devil's ass traps, which means the hazards are above eye level. You can't see them from the fairway.

"I farmed this land from 1956 to '77," he said. "Betty's family, the Herrs, farmed it before that—livestock, produce, a big operation. Betty and I grew up in a day when there was lots of farm help. I was the third of nine kids, and there were twelve in her family. But times have changed. We have just our son, Charlie; we lost another son in his late teens. That's not enough to run a farm, so we started the restaurant and later built the golf course. Betty ran the restaurant for many years before Charlie took over. He studied at the Culinary Institute of America."

Soon Blank and Abe Groff had turned the talk to dairy farming. With the keenness of golfers remembering Sam Snead or Arnold Palmer, they recalled a Holstein stud bull named Osborndale Ivanhoe. "His semen is still available," Blank said. "I visited a farm in the Abruzzi region of Italy not long ago, and they had some in storage there."

Presently Betty Groff drove up. "I've been getting stuff for tomorrow's shoot," she said. "Sorry to keep you boys waiting." One did not mind waiting for such a lively original. She nudged Blank. "Unlike big-time chefs," she said, "I don't go around in whites because I don't have a formal degree, just an 'M-R-S' from when I married Abe. But I've always known my way around food. As a young girl, I raised my own chickens for pocket money. I helped bake bread for the farm; we made fourteen loaves twice a week. I milked cows, worked in the gardens and orchards, even caught fish for the table. Mother never forced me to cook. I got lured into the kitchen by the cooking smells and hearing my mother and aunt talk and laugh. I'd stop to see what was going on. They'd explain what they were making, and then Mother would say casually, 'The celery needs chopping,' or, 'Maybe you'd like to knead this dough.' I was like that dough in her hand."

A little after seven the next morning, we reported to the Groffs' kitchen in a roomy old house near the center of Mount Joy. We were not due until eight, but Blank had risen with the chickens and promptly knocked on my door.

"Good," said Betty. "You're here ahead of the producer. Maybe he'll understand the farm work ethic some day. I don't want to sound mean, but if you bought that man for what he's worth and sold him for what he *thinks* he's worth, you'd make a million."

Blank and I were asked to de-vein spinach, not my favorite task but one I could do. To pass the time, he and Betty did phone skits. He was Bette Davis imperiously ordering booze: a case of Scotch, a case of gin, a bottle of vermouth. She was a Pennsylvania Dutch restaurant hostess giving directions to a city slicker: "When you come to our lane, go in. If the lights aren't on, light the kerosene."

Blank remarked to me, out of Betty's hearing, that he thought her kitchen was not very well organized. He recalled a dinner she had cooked at the Beard House in New York; then, as now, things were a bit helter-skelter. "Cooking in someone else's kitchen," he said, "is like wearing someone else's underwear. But I have to remind myself that Jim Beard loved Betty's informality, even her ditziness. You know, she once played the trumpet in her restaurant."

For myself, I was at home in Betty Groff's overabundance of utensils and ingredients. When asked to find bay leaves, I rooted happily in the familiar clutter. This was not a mere cooking show set but a real kitchen, full of the excess every home cook accumulates.

Esther Press McManus was another of Blank's close women friends. One day, just after he had finished a live cooking demonstration at WHYY, a taped show, "Baking with Julia," appeared on a studio monitor. Julia Child was standing beside a slender, animated woman with a French accent. Julia's companion was making croissants.

"There's Esther," Blank said, giving the woman's name a French pronunciation: Ess-tair. "She lives here in Philadelphia. I adore her. She once came to the restaurant and showed me how to make soufflés." Blank gave me her phone number for a project I was researching. A man answered when I called. "Is Esther there?" I asked "If she were here, you wouldn't be talking to me," he said as if addressing a simpleton. He deigned to take a message, and Esther called back. She would be teaching a baking class at the Restaurant School, she said, and I was welcome to sit in.

"That was her husband, Charlie McManus," Blank explained. "He's a bit of a curmudgeon, but I don't think he's malicious."

As before, I entered the Restaurant School's Italianate manor house in West Philadelphia and proceeded to the new wing of classrooms and kitchens. I found Esther Press McManus in one of the kitchens, talking with a small group of students. She wore a tan skirt and a cotton blouse printed with tiny off-white flowers on a field of black. Her brown hair was medium-length, in what I fancied to be a classic French style.

"This is going to be a small class," she said. "Good. I can give you more attention. Our subject tonight is *brioche*. In France, *brioche* used to be the ultimate gift because it had so many precious ingredients. The enriched dough is unlike any other. It needs to be firm yet soft. But it's capricious and spiteful. It has a terrible memory, only it never forgets your mistake. I always feel when I am making brioche that I am assisting with open-heart surgery—the dough is so tricky."

She began to make the dough while reciting the ingredients— 2½ cups flour, 1 package yeast, 1 teaspoon salt, 2 tablespoons sugar, 2 sticks of butter, 3 to 4 eggs, a little water for the yeast—then carped some more about the pastry's quirky nature. "*Brioche* and I have arguments. We fight all the time. In French it's *la brioche,* so I say I fight with her." The dough is done, she explained, when it comes free from the bowl and wraps around the paddle of the mixer. By then it should have the transparency of paper. After cooling the mixing bowl in ice, she weighed the dough.

"Now that I've mixed this dough," she said, "I can't use it right away because it's not ready. It needs to rise and chill, and that takes many hours. At this stage, I often put the dough in the freezer and use another batch that I've been defrosting in the refrigerator. But your new dough shouldn't go into the freezer naked, without a wash of egg. It's going into a foreign environment after being caressed by your hands, so comfort it with the egg wash. When you defrost frozen dough, be sure to do that in the refrigerator. It should defrost *à coeur,* from the inside out, not the other way."

She examined several doughs she had brought from her home, seeking one that was "young and transparent." Then she rolled it, cautioning about the correct amount of flour: too much makes the rolling slippery, too little may cause the dough to tear. "You have to talk to the dough," she said. "I'm telling it, 'This is what I want you to be,' so that when it goes in the oven, it doesn't go plouf but rises up." She spoke with the zeal of a politician at a rally. "Everything you do with a *brioche* will work for you or against you, one or the other. There is nothing in between."

Students were given dough to roll. One of them, an imposing woman in a turban, seemed hesitant to try. Esther placed her hand on the woman's to show her the rolling motion. I was moved to see her take such care. But then she seemed to have tender feelings for the brioche as well. "When you put the dough in the mold and place it in the oven," she said, "give it some egg wash so it's not all alone in there with only a pilot light. Don't forget, it's going through big changes. The dough you mixed was in its infancy. Now, in the oven, it's in adolescence—that dramatic bloom happens in the oven."

While the brioches baked, Esther showed how to wrap fish in brioche dough. "You can put it right in the freezer," she said, "and when company comes, you put it in the oven. You can also use the dough for *petit pain aux raisins.* I forget the English term."

"Cinnamon buns?" someone suggested.

"Yes. Thank you. Cinnamon buns. If you think brioche is nasty, croissant is even nastier. It has no Christian charity whatsoever. When I was on television, making croissant with Julia Child, I brought with me twenty pieces of dough at different stages of chill. For that one twenty-minute segment, we worked seven hours. The television lights kept heating up the dough."

Soon the *brioches* were ready, enough to eat there and still more to take home. Esther broke off the head of one. "In France we always eat the head first. If a child gives you the head of her brioche, she has to really love you a lot. Remember, if you go to France, brioche are sold in the morning, and eaten with butter. You can also have a delicious glass of water with a little lemon."

One day I called on Esther in the kitchen of her house not far from Rittenhouse Square, the most fashionable of William Penn's five small civic parks. I worried I might run afoul of the acerbic Charles McManus, but if he was at home, he must have been in a distant room. The house, a Victorian brownstone, was big enough to have quartered the French consulate for a time. Its architect, George Hewitt, had been a partner of Frank Furness, the designer of the brownstones that Deux Cheminées occupied. Hewitt also designed the Bellevue-Stratford Hotel, the French Renaissance-style landmark on Broad Street.

I followed Esther from the entry downstairs to her kitchen. Like Blank, she cooked in a nineteenth-century basement, though her workspace opened onto a garden and had many more homelike touches.

"My home town was Marrakesh," Esther said. "I was raised there and in Marseilles, the youngest of thirteen. My mother, like many Moroccan women of her time, did not read. That didn't affect her cooking because Morocco had no cookbooks. I still feel my mother in me, telling the women kneading the bread, 'Just a little more.' It was a cuisine of women. Even today, the chef of the king is a woman. Moroccan cuisine is also about time and company. I like to say, 'The longer it takes, the better it is.' And if you're going to spend time cooking, you'd better have companions. I'm convinced that more people don't cook these days because there's no one to do it with. In Morocco, the maid has a maid has a maid, and so on. My mother always had two people behind her when she shopped.

"When I came to this country as a young woman, I was innocent about working. I just knew I wanted to do something pioneering, something I didn't know how to do. It was the early '70s, and Kathleen Mulhern was planning to start a restaurant. She found a building and she found me. I made a fruit tart for her, and she asked me to be her baker. Six months later, I was her chef. Kathleen sent me to France to learn. At Le Pactole, the Paris restaurant where I trained, I would work until one in the morning and then I would spend until 4 a.m. talking on the phone to Kathleen. She was serious about food. I once made a dough for her seventy-two times before she approved it. For the first year with her, I don't think I saw the sun set or rise."

The Garden, which Mulhern started, became a mainstay of the city's restaurant renaissance. Esther worked there three years before being invited to run the much-bigger kitchen at the Barclay, one of the city's principal hotels.

"The Barclay was a nightmare," she said. "On Fridays before the orchestra performed, we would serve five hundred. I had no experience working with such large quantities, and the men under me didn't like taking orders from a woman. I was there a year. I was rescued by Joe DiLullo, who called to tell me he was opening a restaurant. 'I have an airplane,' he said, 'and I don't know how to fly it.' I asked him, 'What kind of food?' He said, 'Italian.' I told him, 'I don't know it.' 'I ate your food,' he said, 'and I want you to do it. I'll send you to study with Marcella Hazan.' So Joe sent me and my sous chef, Aliza Green, to Marcella's school in Bologna. Aliza is a fabulous cook with a wonderful, wonderful palate. The school itself we didn't like so much. It was for rich ladies, not us. Marcella thought she had two dishwashers. We cleaned more plates and scrubbed more floors than any other chefs alive. It taught me to be nice. I decided I would never be mean again. But then we got sent to a place where we watched pasta being made. Oh, Sam, I wish I could tell you what it was like to walk into a room and see seven women working at a huge table. It was like the House of Dior, like couturiers making the finest clothes. They would throw the pasta with their entire bodies. Aliza and I would be at the doorstep at seven every morning to see them start."

Esther spent only a short time at DiLullo Centro. But Aliza Green stayed on, and during her tenure, it became one of the city's most-popular restaurants. Esther had been lured away to run the kitchen of the Philadelphia Club, a block or so from Deux Cheminées. "I learned to cook for American men," she said. "Pepper pot soup, kidney and veal pie, rice pudding. I made the best rice pudding in the world. These were the sorts of dishes they were accustomed to, from the repertoire of their black servants at home. The first day I came, I eliminated the steam table. I would make anything they wanted if they would call the day before. But often it was like speaking a different language. The members didn't want to pay more than $5 for lunch, so I really had to learn to cook. I think about half of the men appreciated me and half didn't. It was frustrating because I wanted them all to like me. But the kitchen was closed on weekends and holidays, so I had Saturday nights free for the first time in seven years. And I had the whole month of August off.

"After three and a half years at the Philadelphia Club, I wanted to do something on my own. I started a cooking school but found it the most thankless job in the world. Then I catered and consulted. For three years, I was the chef at a restaurant on the shores of Lake Champlain, near Burlington, Vermont. It was open from May to early November. Sam, if ever there was a dream place, this was it for me. I shopped in Montreal, ninety minutes away. Early in the morning, I would go for a six-mile walk, gathering fruit and nuts. There were huge vines of the sweetest Concord grapes. I once walked home with twenty pounds of cherry tomatoes. Customers could pick berries from the restaurant garden. We were building a wonderful name for ourselves. People came from New York City. Many vacationing on the lake came in their yachts. But the restaurant lasted only three seasons, mainly because the government of Vermont required huge expenditures to satisfy the building codes.

"Then came my passionate involvement with Le Bus, the bakery and cafe that started out in a school bus, serving food to Penn students. Now Le Bus makes nearly a hundred varieties of breads and pastries for hundreds and hundreds of stores and restaurants. Can you believe it? I'm lucky to have been involved in so many parts of making food. I can bake bread, make dessert, and cook a decent meal. I can do everything but ice carving."

Another day, Esther invited me back to the Restaurant School. She would be filling in for Robert Bennett, the pastry chef at Le Bec-Fin.

"I am very sorry you are not going to have Bobby Bennett," she told the class. "For my money, he is the best pastry chef, certainly in this country. But he is burned out. He has too many things happening. I can teach most of the things he might have talked about tonight, just don't ask me to decorate anything because I don't know how. In any case, I am going to discuss puff pastry. The French call it *feuilletage or mille feuilles,* referring to the many layers of pastry and butter. You can use the pastry to enclose anything you want—fish, chicken, vegetables. I put the filled pastries in my freezer and take them out when company comes. I do things in stages like that because I never have a whole hour that belongs to me."

She told a story of a poor baker who stole butter from his employer which he took home and hid in a piece of dough before going to bed. Later, his mother took the dough and rolled it, unaware of the butter inside. She folded the dough repeatedly, then threw it in the oven, where it went crazy.

Esther put butter in an envelope of dough and pounded it with a long, handle-less rolling pin. "Don't forget, when you put the butter in the dough, the temperatures of the two must be the same. Dough remembers everything—what you did to it five hours ago or fifteen hours ago—and is unforgiving. If you don't do it right, it takes its revenge. I find that the biggest problem I have with my workers in the restaurant and the bakery is they don't know how to roll. So when you roll, do not allow the dough to move. You must be in control." What an unlikely disciplinarian, I thought, this petite woman with fine French manners.

Soon the students and I were busy pounding and rolling. I heard Esther only in snatches:

"It's a gluten—it's either relaxed or it's not."

"Croissant is a puff pastry with another disease—it's called yeast."

"Dough doesn't like heat or air. Store it with a piece of wrapping on top. I'm stingy with everything except this."

"*Galette des Rois,* with almond cream, is traditionally served during Twelfth Night celebrations."

"*Vol-au-vent*, which means flying in the wind, is a light pastry shell you can fill with vegetables."

"*Palmier,* which is palm leaves in French, is sometimes called pig's ear. This is a puff pastry that is caramelized."

"*Chausson* is a small puff pastry like an apple turnover. French children, after school, would make a beeline for the patisserie to buy one. You would kill your mother for one, or else sell her."

"Some of these pastries might seem hard to make, but I think none is more difficult than American apple pie."

Before the class ended, Esther surprised us with a credible imitation of Julia Child—"more butter, please; put in more butter"—and suggested once more that we use puff pastry to prepare meals in advance. "Why do something ahead of time? Because when the guests come, you're out of your mind. Or you want to spend more time with them and less with the stove. I never finish anything until the guests are sitting down, even if that means taking the meal out of the freezer and putting it in the oven. That way, you have *mise en place,* everything in order."

She paused a few moments and shrugged. "I am obsessed," she said, "with flour and water and its infinite varieties."

8.

The City of
Falling Signs

*I*WAS WALKING one day on Broad Street, central Philadelphia's north-south axis, thinking about the city's vacillating fortunes. For Blank and his colleagues in the restaurant business, and especially women pioneers like Kathleen Mulhern, Esther Press McManus, and Susanna Foo, success has been slow and uncertain—one step back for every two ahead, you might say. Passing the Bellevue-Stratford Hotel, I remembered, as many Philadelphians of my age habitually do, the terrible setback for the renascent city that occurred in 1976 when more than two hundred members of the American Legion, in town for the nation's bicentennial, fell ill with an unidentified pneumonia. Thirty-four died. The Legionnaires had been staying at the Bellevue, a French Renaissance-style relic of the Gilded Age at Broad and Walnut Streets. In its heyday, the Bellevue had been one of the smartest hotels in the nation, with more than a thousand guest rooms, three ballrooms, two resident orchestras, and a rose garden on the roof. The outbreak of "Legionnaires' Disease," as it came to be called in the global media, was devastating to the hotel and the city.

One of the first scientists to study a live culture of the pernicious bacteria was Fritz Blank, thirty-two, chief of clinical microbiology at the Crozer-Chester Medical Center. Blank and his associates, under the auspices of the Centers for Disease Control, labored for months to replicate the pesky bug, as Blank called it. He ran monthly seminars to discuss findings, including one that drew an audience of twelve hundred. After six months, the CDC announced that the culprit had been isolated, identified, and given a name. *Legionella pneumophila,* they said, had spawned in turbid water in the Bellevue's cooling system. We now know that *Legionella* is not peculiar to Philadelphia. In the years since its tragic appearance at the Bellevue, it has been identified in many parts of the world, and government health agencies have established procedures for cooling systems to prevent its occurrence. Yet the notion lingered that the city was unclean, pestilential, a place to avoid. Years passed before the Bellevue resumed profitable operations and Philadelphia's convention business revived.

Other setbacks included demoralizing raids on the city's artistic patrimony. A wall sculpture by the color field artist Ellsworth Kelly, an assemblage of multicolored panels sixty-four feet long, had been installed in the lobby of a downtown office building in 1957. It was the first abstract art to be displayed in a public space in Philadelphia. In 1996, the enormous work somehow vanished, to the dismay of the local art establishment. The building's owner, it turned out, had sold it to a New York art dealer for $100,000. The sculpture then passed, for $1 million, to a New Yorker who placed it on display in the Museum of Modern Art.

"I was shocked and amazed to find it was in New York," said Anne d'Harnoncourt, director of the Philadelphia Museum of Art. "It never occurred to me that it could be removed or moved. Never." A representative of the Museum of Modern Art, bemused by the controversy, offered Philadelphians scant comfort. "New York is not very far away," she said.

The city grew more vigilant. Several years after the Kelly sculpture disappeared, *The Dream Garden,* the Parrish-Tiffany mosaic that had adorned the lobby of the Curtis Building since 1916, and which I had seen every day during my time at the *Saturday Evening Post,* nearly ended up in a Las Vegas hotel. This time, intervention through the courts and the Philadelphia Historical Commission kept *The Dream Garden* in place. A few years later, the city's art community, led by museum director d'Harnoncourt, raised $87 million to prevent removal of Thomas Eakins's *The Gross Clinic,* the best-known work of the city's most eminent artist, to the museum of a Walmart heir in Arkansas.

Perhaps the greatest hindrance to the city's recovery was decay by intention. In the early years of the Restaurant Renaissance, when Georges Perrier and other pioneers were nagging the city to pull up its socks, a real estate speculator named Samuel Rappaport became the prime owner of commercial property in Center City. His portfolio included the Victory Building, designed in the 1870s in Second Empire style. The outside was faced in granite, the interior was an intricacy of columns and pilasters, ironwork and marble. Four blocks from Independence Hall, the Victory Building had been an attraction during the Centennial Exposition of 1876.

Rappaport also held a fifteen-year lease to manage the Reading Terminal Market. At the market, he raised rents 400 percent, imposed new fees on vendors, and made few of the improvements he'd promised. Within two years, more than half of the market's tenants had left, and Rappaport was bought out of the lease.

Meanwhile, the Victory Building languished, occupied only by vagrants. Trash accumulated in the lower floors. Sumac trees grew from the fifth-floor windows. After ignoring the building for nearly twenty years, Rappaport sought permission to demolish it. "I'm deathly afraid that one of those curlicues and faces will fall and kill somebody," he told the Department of Licenses and Inspections. The department agreed, but preservationists intervened. The Victory Building was purchased for $1.1. million, restored for $20 million, and made into residences with ceilings fifteen feet high and floors of the original marble.

Rappaport died in 1994, leaving more than fifty buildings in the care of his estate. One of them was a three-story garage not far from Deux Cheminées that had been built in the 1920s. On a Sunday afternoon in October 1997, Judge Berel Caesar of the Court of Common Pleas was walking past the garage when a five hundred-pound sign became dislodged and fell to the street, along with five tons of brick. Caesar was killed. In court, lawyers for his family cited a 1991 engineer's report, ordered by Rappaport himself, that called the structure "unsuitable for continued use in the present function without repairs in the immediate future." Attorneys for the Rappaport estate argued that repairs had been made but agreed to settle for $5.25 million.

For those concerned about the viability of the struggling city, the falling sign that killed Judge Caesar symbolized the perfidy of neglect. "We hope building owners and managers will be reminded by the results today that they have an obligation of basic care and decency toward the city and its people," his son said after the settlement. "We hope they remember as well that profit is not the only master to be served."

While some speculators were dealing in blight, another businessman was giving the city a new face. In 1986 Rappaport sold some property to Willard Rouse, whose family had previously built Faneuil Hall Marketplace in Boston and the South Street Seaport in Manhattan. Rouse broke the custom that no building should exceed 548 feet, the height of the Philadelphia City Hall tower and its crowning ornament, a twenty-seven-ton statue of William Penn. Rouse's One Liberty Place, designed by the German-American architect Helmut Jahn, caused predictable controversy at first, but the city grew to like the shimmering spire that rose more than four hundred feet above Penn's cast-iron hat. Other towers followed, including two more by Rouse and his partners. "These skyscrapers have given the city a real skyline," Paul Goldberger wrote in the *New York Times*. "And by happy circumstance, the buildings are sufficiently well spaced to permit them to be seen from the street as well as from afar; they do not crowd each other so tightly that they blur into a granite and glass mush, as happens in much of midtown Manhattan. The truly special thing here, and the reason this city's recent crop of mega-skyscrapers has so far had a more benign effect than in many cities, is Philadelphia's unusual streetscape of three- and four-story buildings, many of them right in the shadow of the largest towers. The real key to the architecture of this downtown is the way in which its two worlds—the skyscrapers and the smaller buildings of the street—coexist, melding together to give the city its identity and its spirit."

The mix Goldberger spoke of suits the civic taste for buildings of modest scale, as a foil to grandeur, and for weathered stone and brick as a counterpoint to glossy new materials. The Kimmel Center for the Performing Arts, which opened in 2001, is liked well enough for its ambitious design by Rafael Viñoly, and for its perky acoustics, but it will never displace the public's affection for the Academy of Music, the dowager which was completed in 1857 and is the oldest functioning concert hall in the nation. Farther up Broad Street, the callow elevations of the Pennsylvania Convention Center, begun in the 1990s and expanded a decade later, are tempered by much-older neighbors: the Furness-designed Pennsylvania Academy of the Fine Arts (1876); the Reading Terminal and its great vaulting train shed (1893), and eight blocks of bustling, exotically odorous, often-unkempt Chinatown.

Buffeted for decades by decline and renewal, progress and backsliding, Philadelphians have developed a what-have-we-got-to-lose outlook that frees them to speak without inhibition. When the host of a combative TV talk show visited the city to recruit opinionated everymen for his program, he praised Philadelphians for being "very aware, savvy. They know the issues. They're good for us because they're not afraid to get in the face of the person they think is wrong, even if they just met them in the lobby." That will not come as news to athletes, umpires, and referees who displease the city's boo-bird spectators. Even a Russian pianist was once booed off the stage by a Philadelphia Orchestra audience for playing too slowly.

It is not widely known beyond the city limits that a young Philadelphian with such get-in-your-face tendencies played an important part in the legal fracas that nearly brought Bill Clinton's presidency to an early end. The story begins with Richard Marcus, an entrepreneur of sorts who created and marketed a minimally processed peanut butter he called Crazy Richard's. "Crazy" Richard Marcus had two sons, one of whom became an architect in New York and an advocate for gay rights. The other studied law at the University of Chicago and went to work for Berger & Montague, a Philadelphia firm whose principals were active in national Democratic politics. Within his family, not to mention his law firm, Jerome was something of an anomaly. "His brother was called 'Benjie,'" a former neighbor of the Marcus family told me, "but you would never call Jerome 'Jerry.' He was intense and very serious, a Jewish exclusivist in the mold of Benjamin Netanyahu." Another acquaintance told a reporter, "He looks kind of like an obsessed person. I see him on the street sometimes, muttering to himself." Still another remembered his eccentric behavior in law school. "He would shriek things out in the middle of class. Most students learn the rules after a while and raise their hands. Jerome never did. Professors liked him, but he drove them nuts. He just didn't know when to stop."

One can only guess what Marcus muttered to himself on the streets of Philadelphia, but in the mid-1990s, it was likely he had Bill Clinton on his mind, a man he accused, in print, of being puny, debauched, a criminal. Through Richard Porter, a law school classmate who worked in the law firm of Kenneth Starr, Marcus agreed to help in the sexual harassment lawsuit brought against Clinton by Paula Jones. Sub rosa, Marcus wrote briefs and complaints that helped to advance Jones's case. Then, in a conference call in January 1998 with Porter and New York literary agent Lucianne Goldberg, Marcus learned of an affair between the president and Monica Lewinsky. He arranged a dinner in Philadelphia with Porter and Paul Rosenzweig, another classmate from law school. Rosenzweig traveled up from Washington, where he was on the staff of Starr, who had become the independent counsel investigating the Clintons. The three men met for dinner at Deux Cheminées, an easy walk from Marcus's workplace. One would like to have been an eavesdropping waiter that evening, but who knew? Did Blank visit their table? He doesn't remember. Men in suits talking *sotto voce* in his restaurant weren't uncommon. "If I'd known what they were up to," Blank said, "I could have poisoned their soup."

Back in Washington the next day, Rosenzweig passed the Lewinsky tip to his cohorts in the independent counsel's office. In the end, as we know, Clinton was acquitted in an impeachment trial before the U.S. Senate. One of those voting to acquit was Senator Arlen Specter, a Philadelphia resident and friend of the Marcus family. No slouch himself at getting in the face of foes and friends, Specter voted against the wishes of his party because, as he said, the Senate trial had been piecemeal and a sham. Though Jerome Marcus had not succeeded in driving President Clinton from office, he at least had stirred up troubles that stuck to the wheels of government like peanut butter.

Blank was not surprised when he learned of the furtive meeting of Clinton foes at his restaurant. "Everything passes through this town," he said. "Stuff may not begin or end in Philadelphia, but everyone and everything passes through at one time or another. Do you know what a bursa is?"

"No," I said. "It sounds anatomical."

"Well, in birds you have T-cells that convert to B-cells by passing through the bursa, or bursa of Fabricius. Philadelphia is like the bursa of the world. Everything and everyone passes through. Do you remember when the president of China came to the U.S. last year? He made a special stop two blocks from here to visit a retired Penn professor who taught him math in Shanghai back in the

1940s. The professor came to the U.S. in 1950, but he's still remembered in China as a national treasure. Who would ever guess such a fellow was living in a little apartment up the street?"

Not many months after the Lewinsky hubbub subsided, Philadelphia learned that it had been chosen to host the 2000 Republican convention. Mayor Ed Rendell had worked hard to entice either political party to come, and there was a celebratory mood when he made the sale. Inevitably, there was booing, too. "I don't see how all this is going to help what ails Philadelphia," the *Inquirer's* business columnist wrote. "The city's tax structure repels business. It's losing middle-class families because of schools and crime. Vast sections of town are crumbling for lack of private investment. Bureaucracy, monopolies, and labor rules make entrepreneurship a nightmare. And having eight thousand politicians here for a week is supposed to improve things? What am I missing?"

He was missing the salutary fact that, after the debacle of 1948, Philadelphia now had enough hotel rooms for a major event. And restaurants like Deux Cheminées and Le Bec-Fin could expect a week or two of intense business during the otherwise-slow month of August—not to mention television coverage across the nation that would raise the city's profile, stimulate tourism, and attract more conventions.

As it turned out, business during the Republican convention was only so-so for Deux Cheminées and most other restaurants. The convention was held in a distant sports complex at the south end of the city. When delegates were not on the convention floor or being bussed to and from their hotels, they ate catered meals under a big tent close by the convention facility. However, a lunch was held at Deux Cheminées for the wives of Republican VIPs.

"They were a pretty snooty, self-important bunch, according to the waiters," Blank said. "I have to admit, most of the waiters don't follow politics, so they might have annoyed some of the women by not knowing who they were, by not kowtowing enough. When some of the boys watched the news that evening, they saw one of the ladies from the lunch, on stage with the nominee. They said, 'Oh, there's that woman from lunch, still in that dress.' It was Laura Bush, of course. Leave it to a Deux Cheminées waiter to recognize a political celebrity by *that dress.*'"

Blank, a man of sense and science, had a larger civic matter to fret about than conspirators and conventioneers at his tables. The section of Camac Street that ran past his delivery door was paved in wood, and that wood had disintegrated. Wood is an odd and impractical material for a modern city street, but in 1910, not long after the townhouses at 1221 Locust were built, wood blocks were installed to reduce the din made by horses and carriages on stone. From 1910 to 1920 some twenty miles of Philadelphia streets, including little Camac, were surfaced in pine and oak. But the wood on the main thoroughfares soon disintegrated from rot and the pounding of traffic. On hot days city streets reeked of horse urine that had penetrated the wood. When automobiles began to appear in the 1920s, the wooden paving was replaced with asphalt, except for a four hundred-foot section of Camac between Locust and Walnut. There, along the brick west wall of Deux Cheminées, the wood stayed in reasonably good condition for the better part of the twentieth century. But decay set in at last, aggravated by utility crews rooting in the street and patching the holes they made with blacktop. Because this little stretch of Camac was the last remnant of wood paving in the city, $350,000 was allocated to install new wood blocks. "It's really an interesting little street," said the Streets Department's chief engineer. "It's kind of a neat project, too." Blank welcomed the news. He had always wanted to run a Viennese-style street cafe in the slow summer months, and a refurbished Camac might make that possible.

The project was announced in springtime. Completion was expected by winter. But the city had trouble finding a mill that could supply oak blocks in the quantity required. The work ran a year over schedule, prompting a newspaper to jeer that an eight-mile stretch of I-76, the Schuylkill Expressway, had been resurfaced in less time. For all those months, trucks making deliveries to Deux Cheminées maneuvered through construction debris or else unloaded far from Blank's service door. Even when the repaving was completed (in theory) and the street crews moved on, many of the new blocks popped out and lay on the street like dislodged teeth.

Though Gorse, his main partner, scotched Blank's idea for a street cafe, the chef believed the city should finish the repaving properly, so he wrote to the district engineer with several common-sense suggestions. Today, thanks in good measure to Blank's nagging, the only wooden street in Philadelphia—perhaps the only such street in the nation—is in reasonably good repair and attracts occasional tourists for its novelty.

In many ways, it represents the city's well-meant, if halting, effort to keep its past while serving the present. "OK, so it doesn't sound so exciting to visit a street for the actual street itself," said a tourism website, "but one block of Camac is supposedly the last and only wooden street in the city. We're not talking about planks or hardwood flooring here—just hundreds of wooden blocks wedged tightly into place. It's a public street, so go whenever you like. But try to avoid days when the surface is wet. The wood blocks get slippery, and you might just fall on your ass."

Winespotting

*I*N AN UNDERGROUND RECESS, fenced and gated, the wine cellar at Deux Cheminées was well away from most kitchen activities. Blank no longer drank alcohol and seldom spoke of wine in his classes. He did instruct on the use of alcohol in cooking—vermouth in dishes that called for white wine, cognac in poultry basting, sherry and Scotch in certain soups, and so on—but there was no discussion of pairing wines with food, or anything else from the vast lore of wine.

Neil Gorse bought the wine for the restaurant. He would study the numerical ratings in the wine magazines and try to pair high scores with low prices. That was a challenge, since Pennsylvania's state-run wholesale and retail monopoly, the Liquor Control Board (LCB), set prices that were generally higher than in neighboring New Jersey and Delaware. "The state store system makes it hard for restaurants here," Aliza Green told me. "In most places in America, you can make up for high food costs with the wine markup. You'd think we could change it here, but there's strong resistance. Pennsylvania is the biggest buyer of wine in the world, and the account holders, the brokers who provide the wine to the LCB, are unbelievably powerful."

In addition to price, there was the issue of limited selection. The wines available to restaurants through the Liquor Control Board were generally those of the largest international producers whose aim was mass appeal. One taste fit all, you might say.

Georges Perrier's Le Bec-Fin was an exception. I could not afford to eat there often, but when I did, I encountered some uncommon wines that were sensibly priced. Meals began with Champagne from houses unfamiliar to me: Diebolt-Vallois, Trianon, and l'Esperance. Nor had I heard of most other vintners on Perrier's list, such as Poniatowski from the Loire, Bonhomme or Ampeau from Burgundy, Isola e Olena from Tuscany. The sommelier, quiet and efficient, was a man of forty or so who cut a good figure in his tuxedo. He understood right away—seemed pleased, in fact—that I wanted good wine for a modest price. I asked him how he managed to buy in such variety through the state store system. "Actually, you can get almost any wine you want through the Liquor Control Board," he said, "but you have to do the research so you know what to order. I actually visit the small wine makers, in France primarily. It helps that I've learned French while working for Chef Perrier."

Not many months later, I found myself at a big round table in the upstairs dining room of London Grille, a dependable neighborhood restaurant not far from the art museum. There were five such tables in the room, each one bristling with wine glasses. Through a window I could see the sooty walls of Eastern State Penitentiary, once the *beau ideal* of Victorian-era punishment, now a prison museum. I had come to hear a series of talks on wine offered through the same University of Pennsylvania program that sponsored Chef Blank's classes. The instructor would be the sommelier of Le Bec-Fin, Gregory Moore. While learning to cook, I reckoned, I should learn more about wine. It was high time.

In my early years, the men in my family had just two table duties besides holding the women's chairs: carving the roast and pouring the wine. Slim, my father, did not like to carve, so as soon as I was old enough to handle a knife, I was deployed to the sideboard to have at the turkey or standing rib or leg of lamb. Slim did not much care for wine either. The cocktails he and my mother drank before dinner were brought to the table and nursed. Sparkling wine appeared at holidays, and every so often, we might have a Portuguese rosé in a funny pinch bottle or else red wine from California claiming to be Burgundy.

To be fair to my father, good wine was not generally available in America in the 1940s and '50s, at least not in the Pennsylvania countryside. Later, on college weekends in the late 1950s, Risa and I made picnics of French bread, Danish cheese, and *liebfraumilch,* a German white with an alluring nun on the label but not much character. Then, a few years after graduation, while a very junior magazine editor on assignment in Texas, I encountered, in a Houston restaurant, a white wine from France that was far superior to any wine I had tasted before. It was bright and fresh and gave me the sense of having walked from gloom into sunlight. I didn't record the name of the vineyard, but the word *Graves* on the label stayed in my memory. Graves, I found out later, was not a French cemetery but the *appellation* (since renamed Pessac-Leognan) of Domaine de Chevalier and Chateau Haut Brion, which in the 1960s, were among the few producers of good white Bordeaux.

Through the decades that followed, I encountered enough good wine to develop a notion of what to choose from a list. But I hardly knew what I was doing. The first time Risa and I had dinner at Deux Cheminées and Blank came to our table, we ordered a Château Cheval Blanc because we had few opportunities to drink a first-growth Bordeaux. I was also seduced by the wine's high numerical rating, bestowed by *Wine Spectator* and printed on Deux Cheminées' list. Our Cheval Blanc might have deserved its high mark eventually, but just then, four years from its vintage, it was too young—as tight as a rubber band, to borrow an expression from the restaurant critic Moira Hodgson. I should have known better.

Moore arrived shortly before the class was to start, looking rather collegiate in a blue blazer and button-down shirt. He was a little breathless but all business as he made swift preparations, assuring himself that all the wines we were to taste had been chilled to his satisfaction, the reds as well as the whites. He struck me as a taller and more serious rendition of another man with the same last name, the English actor Dudley Moore.

"Wine," he began, "is the fermented juice of the wine grape *Vitis vinifera.* Within that single species are three thousand or so grape varietals, including the few we'll look at tonight. Left alone, grape juice naturally ferments into vinegar, so the object of viniculture is to control that process."

Bottles of German and Alsatian Riesling were distributed to the tables. We detected, under Moore's direction, *le goût de pétrole,* Riesling's characteristic hint of gasoline. Moore regarded his own glass in the manner of a chemist examining a beaker, tilting and swirling to coat the inside, sniffing, holding it to the light and then sniffing again. Presently he sipped and made the wine taster's exaggerated chewing motions with his mouth. "Wine transforms with time, inside its container," he said. "I like to track its evolution in the glass. I don't let it just sit there until it 'opens.'"

It wasn't long before Moore had warmed to his subject, and my handwritten notes became less legible. "Wine tells me that God loves me," he said, reverently appraising a Mosel Valley *qualitätswein mit prädikat.* Rising up on his toes, he added, "I love to drink German wines in the summer." The wines we had already tasted and our anticipation of the grapes to come—the pinot noirs, the syrahs, and the nebbiolos—had something to do with the growing mood of effervescence in the room, but most of the excitement came from Moore himself. "Great wines reflect the character of their *terroir,* their place of origin," he said. "Before the world wars drove the German market down, Rieslings were the highest expression of *terroir,* valued above the wines of Bordeaux. Now they're bargains. A $16 Riesling from the Mosel is of much better quality than a $16 California chardonnay."

Having dispatched the Rieslings, we proceeded to pinot noir. Red wine is usually served too warm in restaurants, Moore said; in fact, 50 percent of the Burgundy sold in this country is heat damaged. He placed two cooled bottles on each table. One was from California's Carneros district, the other from the vineyards of Morey St. Denis, in Burgundy's Côte de Nuits. Moore tasted both, and we followed suit. "The tastes of dark cherries and clove are

common to the grape," Moore said, "though the varietal charac-
teristics of pinot noir are more elusive than Riesling's *goût de pétrole*.
You'll notice that the French wine is more complex. The difference
is like hung game versus Perdue chicken. That's because Burgundy's climate is continental, with a much-longer growing season
than in maritime California."

The class forged on, from pinot noir to syrah from the Rhone
Valley's Côte Rôti ("Syrah can mature in the bottle for twenty
years," Moore said) and the nebbiolo grape ("difficult to grow prof-
itably") from the Piedmont region of Italy. The following week we
appraised chardonnay ("one of the most versatile of noble wines")
in various permutations: Champagne blanc de blanc, several California versions, Chablis ("naked, unadorned chardonnay, never
touched by oak"), and even a chardonnay from Tuscany. The star
of the second evening was a sixteen-year-old Meursault from
Michel Ampeau. "Most producers in Burgundy sell out their
whites within two years of harvest," Moore said, "but Ampeau's
wines, when that young, are green and hard and inscrutable. Ampeau cellars his whites for up to ten years before releasing them to
market." Moore swirled his glass, inspected, sniffed, tasted. "The
nobility of chardonnay is only revealed by bottle aging," he said.
"Wines like this are a privilege to drink."

It was also a privilege to drink, in the final class, a 1989 Léoville
Barton. The wines of Bordeaux are not a complete varietal, Moore
explained, because they are blended, typically 70 percent cabernet
sauvignon softened by 20 percent merlot and 10 percent cabernet
franc. "Pure cabernet sauvignon can be tough and tannic," he said.
"It's for people who like a little pain with their pleasure." Maybe
so, but I got no pain from the three California cabernets he poured
for us. They were from Rutherford Bench in the Napa Valley ("I
taste mint and eucalyptus," Moore said), Paso Robles in San Luis
Obispo County ("Mmmm, chocolate"), and Santa Maria Valley in
Santa Barbara County ("Very aristocratic and European, with balanced fruit and structure").

When he wasn't commenting on the wine in his glass, Moore peppered us with general observations.

On cultivation: "The job of the grower is to provide the conditions for the wine to become itself. Grapes don't like their roots to soak, so they do well in river valleys with good drainage. Also, slopes protect against wind that would rob grapes of moisture."

On the market: "Unfortunately, some grape varieties with the potential to make great wines will become extinct because of the market's drive toward homogeneity. Too many vineyards are planted in chardonnay and cabernet sauvignon, when some other variety would be more appropriate."

On cellaring: "Wine is a perishable commodity, like milk, and routinely subjected to abuse in transport and storage. So it's best to buy it young and store yourself. But don't leave it there and forget it. We bow and scrape to bottles as if they're totemic objects. Wine, like people, has something to offer at every stage of life, so you should drink it old and young. It's an agricultural product, not a mutual fund."

On wine with food: "In Italy and France, the more complex the cuisine, the simpler the wine should be that complements it, and vice versa. A complicated dish can sabotage a complex wine. This is a more-reliable rule than white with fish and red with meat."

On ranking wines by number: Moore railed against the practice, which he felt had created a generation of drinkers who knew wine scores but didn't know wine. "It's no good to memorize a bunch of data when you can't evaluate the best evidence of all, the wine in your glass. There are so many variables in the creation and tasting of a wine that it's absurd to give one wine an eighty-four and another an eighty-three and another an eighty-six. What's the difference between them, really? Who can distinguish in such tiny increments? And the rankings have a bad influence on wine making. Too many wines are 'sculpted' to make a big first impression, either for tastings or to wow expense-account restaurant diners. I remember drinking a Barbaresco, from the Piedmont region of

Italy, made by Bruno Giacosa. It went very well with game. *Wine Spectator* had rated it fifty-nine, which is about as low as they go. But all it needed was another year or two in the bottle."

Altogether, I sniffed and sipped through a dozen of Moore's classes, emerging with extensive handwritten notes and a few conclusions of my own. I resolved, for example, to throw away the crutch of numerical ratings, not only for the reasons Greg Moore gave but also for the obsession they could generate. I did not want to spend my days immersed in the pages of *Wine Spectator* and *Wine Advocate,* committing lists of data to memory. I did not want to become a winespotter, a variant of those eccentric folk called trainspotters who stand beside Britain's railway tracks and write down the numbers inscribed on passing trains.

I also resolved to use decent wine in cooking, not the cheapest of the cheap, as I had done. This prompted me to sometimes cook a dish to make use of—perhaps I should say do justice to—the remnant of a good red or white that might be languishing in the fridge. Around the time I attended Moore's classes, I had the opportunity to buy, at a price I could afford, six cases of Château Haut Brion's house wine. At first I fawned over my acquisition, hardly daring to open a bottle. But over the years, as it aged and softened, I became more liberal with it, and finally the day came when I used a cup of it to make my favorite Czech goulash. A sin perhaps, but the dish was delicious, especially with a glass of the same nectar.

Determined to follow Moore's lead, I sought out the unexpected and unconventional on restaurant wine lists. In Columbus, Ohio, I found a *viognier* that added a mellow glow to a remarkable Italian meal. In a country inn far from the beaten path in upstate New York, Risa and I spied a *Vosne-Romanée* and pounced. "I got very drunk," Risa remembered, "and loved every minute of it." At Clarke's, in the Notting Hill district of London, I was surprised to encounter a Frog's Leap zinfandel from Rutherford in the Napa Valley that went perfectly with Chef Sally Clarke's food and made me proud to be a Yank. And in Washington, D.C., I happened on what seemed an oddity at the time—the Chianti grape in a California wine. Risa and I had returned to our hotel, too tired to go out for supper. We begged a table from the hotel's maître d', a tuxedoed fellow with a smooth act.

"No one should be allowed to have so much style as you have," he told my wife as he pulled out her chair.

"You're full of it," she said approvingly.

"That may be so," he said, "but I never lie about appearances."

He took our orders and gave me the wine list. I was almost too weary to make sense of it, but my eye fell on a *sangiovese* from California, a novelty to me. Thanks to Greg Moore, I knew that *sangiovese* was the grape grown in the Chianti region of Tuscany. Recently, while staying with friends near Siena, I'd bought Chianti made at Castello di Volpaia, just up the road from our quarters. That wine, I swear, tasted of the sere Tuscan soil and was just right with a plate of *tagliatelle* with chickpeas and rosemary.

"Let's see how the Californians do *sangiovese*," I told the maître d'.

"An excellent choice," he said. "I think it's my last bottle."

I was skeptical about the "my last bottle" claim, but in fact, the wine was delicious and went beautifully with Risa's rack of lamb and the beans and pasta I ordered in remembrance of my *tagliatelle con ceci* in Tuscany.

The maître d' came by often to chat. "If the chef were an artist," he asked, "who would he be? The last one I had here was Matisse, a master, but I haven't decided about this fellow."

"It's honest food," Risa said. "I'd say Stuart Davis or John Marin."

"Thomas Hart Benton," I volunteered.

As he filled our glasses with the last of the *sangiovese*, I told our new friend what Greg Moore had said about wine being evidence of God's love for humanity. What did he think of that?

His eyebrows shot up. "You're asking me? Before I ran this restaurant, I was a priest. Yes, a priest. I am not joking. So of course I believe that." He pointed to my glass. "And when I pour the wine, you must finish it all."

In the course of attending Greg Moore's wine classes, I learned that his brother David ran a wine shop, Triangle Liquors, in Camden, New Jersey. "Wear old clothes" to go there, someone advised me. The shop was in the small, dusty basement of what might have been an abandoned building. David Moore was affable and busy with customers. He took the time to sell me some Alsatian Riesling and to tell me he was dividing his time between Triangle Liquors and a farm in western Pennsylvania. I was put on the store's mailing list and began to receive a chatty newsletter that soon announced the opening of a new wine store, Moore Brothers, up the road in Pennsauken, Fritz Blank's native turf. Customers were assured that all wine would be shipped to the store in refrigerated conveyances and that the temperature in the store would be kept at 56 degrees year-round.

Chef Perrier expanded his business, as well, opening a second restaurant, which he called Brasserie Perrier, a block from Le Bec-Fin. Risa and I went there for the first time after a performance of the Beaux Arts Trio at the Convention Center. During the concert, my mind wandered as I noticed the trio's roly-poly pianist, Menachem Pressler, moving his mouth in an odd way while he played, as though he might be eating something—or thinking about eating something—delectable. In his white tie, boiled shirt, and tailcoat, he was an epicure of the Gilded Age, so I imagined, dreaming of post-performance champagne and caviar. The notion made me hungry. I said to Risa, "Let's go to Perrier's new place after this is over." At a table near the bar, we drank Muscat and I consumed an abstract tableau of mounded chocolate, pistachio ice cream, a pastry stick, and ornamental dribbles. I was nearly comatose when our waiter told us that Greg Moore would be hosting an upcoming dinner and wine tasting to honor wine makers from France, Italy, and California. We signed on.

Moore's dinner, for about fifty, was held in an upstairs room done smartly in gray fabric and cherry wood. Risa and I sat at a table that included André and Pascal Bonhomme, father and son, whose white burgundy, Macon Viré, was one of the house wines at Le Bec-Fin. The two Frenchmen radiated the vitality of farm life. Their rosy cheeks and Sunday-go-to church tweeds distinguished them from most others in the room, all city pallor and somber dress. We felt at home with them, though our French was halting. We learned that Pascal had an eight-month-old baby back home, and that making wine was entirely a family operation. Their small production—less than five thousand cases a year—yielded too little revenue for hiring workers or advertising. In any case, they said, no one outside the family would want to work their long hours. But why would the Bonhommes need to advertise when Le Bec-Fin and Michelin-starred restaurants in France were already their customers?

After several dishes and wines had been dispatched, a young chef at our table, a member of Les Dames d'Escoffier, declared that she had never been to a wine party of this quality. In addition to the Bonhommes' white burgundy, we had drunk Paolo de Marchi's Tuscan syrah, Steve Storr's Santa Cruz zinfandel, and a Sonoma County cabernet sauvignon by Patrick Campbell of Laurel Glen. Moore stood and introduced the maker as each wine was poured. Toward the end of the meal, as more wines went down, he saluted Brian Talley of Arroyo Grande Valley, Bryan Babcock of Santa Ynez Valley, François Barmes of Barmes Beucher in Alsace, and from Vouvray in the Loire, Prince Philippe Poniatowski.

Many of the wine makers toasted Moore in return. "Philadelphia was my first market outside of California," Babcock said. "When I was first getting started, I took some of my wine to a dealer who worked out of a garage here. Fortunately, the dealer liked what he tasted. 'We're going to Le Bec-Fin,' he said. So we went, and, bingo, I knew Greg fifteen minutes and he told me he was placing an order. It was a pivotal moment."

Near the end, Chef Perrier appeared from the wings, heading for our table. He greeted the Bonhommes warmly and stayed awhile to chat. Then, like an orchestra conductor, he called out the staff to take a bow and shook Moore's hand. "Thank you, Greg," he said, "for enduring twenty years of my screaming and plates on the floor."

Partners

"NEIL PAID FOR THE LIQUOR," Chef Blank told me sotto voce during a fundraising dinner at his restaurant for the Philadelphia Singers, Blank's favorite cause. I understood him to mean that Neil Gorse, Blank's housemate at one time, was being generous to his old friend. Gorse, so I gathered, could afford to pick up a tab like this one. He had profited from the sale of a business he started and had invested the proceeds well. To use a local expression, Gorse was wealthy but didn't live like it. His one extravagance, if you chose to view it that way, was a summer house on the shore of Long Island.

Gorse's thrift, which Blank appeared to share in most respects, influenced Blank's restaurant. Much of the furniture and decor, as well as table settings and kitchen gear, had been bought at auctions and clearance sales. The cloches, for example, the dome-like plate covers that waiters removed ceremonially after delivering food to tables, had been found at a distress sale for failed Atlantic City hotels. The most elegant of the dining room chairs, as Blank had revealed during the Gershwin dinner, had been salvaged from the late Peter von Starck's La Panetière. Even the oil portraits that hung in the parlors and dining rooms of Deux Cheminées, depictions of mostly anonymous gentry, had been obtained from estate sales. This is not to say that Blank was cheap. He was merely frugal in a city that hewed to Franklin's adage that a penny saved is a penny earned. Of all the restaurants in Philadelphia, Deux Cheminées was, to me, the one most characteristic of the city's timeworn appeal. It did not matter that a rug had threadbare places or a mantel clock might not work or that the dignified folk looking down from their portraits had been cast off by their heirs; it all went together to make a homey quintessence of the old city. Indeed, the abandoned portrait subjects had found a new home and place of honor in the patchwork family of Deux Cheminées.

Daytimes at the restaurant, I sometimes saw Gorse in the office, answering the phone, ordering wine for the restaurant cellar, and helping to arrange the special events, corporate and private, that provided much of the restaurant's income. A feisty defender of his friend, Gorse sometimes wrote acerbic letters to counter the infrequent bad review. "Write what you will about this restaurant, dear lady," he told a waspish magazine critic, "all we ask is that you get the facts straight before you loose the dogs." He pointed out half a dozen errors she had made, including inaccurate prices and misidentified food and wine. The magazine published a retraction.

But there were times when Gorse was powerless to defend his pal from public outrage. After a vacation in Sri Lanka, where Blank had been photographed riding an elephant, the chef amused friends back home by circulating the picture along with a tongue-in-cheek recipe for cooking the animal.

Chef's Recipe for Elephant
(Usually takes two to three weeks to prepare)

Ingredients:
Elephant
Large onions, chopped
Rabbits

Method:
Skin and debone the elephant
Make stock from the bones
Cut the elephant into bite-sized pieces
Saute the onion and meat until nicely browned
Make 400 gallons of gravy from the stock, and add to the meat
Simmer in a huge pot for four days
This will serve 3,416 people. If more guests show up, add the rabbits.

After the recipe found its way into the Sunday *Inquirer*, a few readers who failed to get the joke heaped scorn on Blank and the newspaper ("stupid," "insensitive," "nauseating").

One day when Blank was grumbling to me about the ineptitude of a young kitchen worker, he paused and said, "Maybe I shouldn't be so harsh. The kid's not quite thirty. That's a confusing age. It certainly was for me. Thank God I met Neil. It was 1970. I was twenty-seven and sitting in a bar called the Allegro. I had led a pretty cloistered life up to then, even though I was in the Army at the time. I was dressed in civvies and feeling like a fish out of water. I was drinking at the crowded bar and scared to death—you know, clammy hands, cold feet. But I did have the guts to say to the stranger next to me something like, 'Gee, they sure could use another bartender in here.' Well, the stranger was Neil. Pretty soon I was confiding in him, telling him how uncomfortable I was in that place, which, of course, was partly my discomfort at being a soldier on leave in the big city. Neil cut right to the point. He said, 'Everyone's here for the same reason you are, looking for friendship, looking for where they belong.' Before I met Neil, I thought I would never have a meaningful relationship. But then it happened."

Gorse's friendship helped Blank overcome his inhibitions. In the house they shared in Society Hill, Blank cooked the meals and educated Gorse's palate.

"Neil grew up in Altoona," Blank said. "I'm not knocking him or his hometown, but there was a time when Neil thought Kool-Aid was a pretty sophisticated drink. In Society Hill back then, everyone gave dinner parties. In a sense, the city's culinary renaissance started at home. That's how I got started, making four dinner parties a week. It wasn't that big a jump from four weekly parties to the idea of opening a restaurant. If the restaurant didn't work out, I figured, I could always go back to my lab job at the medical and burn center, saving lives and stomping out disease."

The first Deux Cheminées, on Camac Street, was a stone's throw from the present location. Blank found a house for himself on Camac as well, a typical nineteenth-century "trinity"—three floors with essentially one room per floor. The kitchen, which he renovated over time, was so small he had to place a cutting board over the sink to create counter space. But he was seldom there. A typical day at the restaurant ran from 6 a.m. to 11 p.m., with few days off. There was just one stove, but, as Blank remembered, "life was simpler then, and there was more camaraderie among chefs and restaurants—none of this snooty 'I work at Le Bec-Fin.'"

The restaurant opened in 1979, and was an immediate hit, helped by a favorable review in the *Inquirer* from Elaine Tait. Success kept the small staff so busy that no one had time to tend the books. Bills and receipts just piled up on the office desk. When Blank and Gorse finally totaled things up, they discovered they were losing money at the rate of about $10 a customer.

"We didn't panic," Blank said. "In fact, we probably helped ourselves in the long run by mistakenly undercharging. It established our clientele, and when we gradually raised prices to get ourselves into the black, no one seemed to mind."

In the beginning, the restaurant served lunch as well as dinner. "It killed me, in such a small kitchen," Blank said. "We stopped after a year. Too few customers from the business district were willing to cross Broad Street to have lunch."

For six years, the restaurant flourished at the Camac Street location. Then one August night in 1987, the phone rang in Blank's house.

"I had been up late drinking and didn't pick up in time. I assumed it was a routine call from the alarm company. The alarm system at the restaurant was oversensitive, and I often got called when it went off at night."

Minutes later the phone rang again. This time Blank got it. Someone said, "The firemen are there." He reached the scene just as Gorse arrived, too. Deux Cheminées was ruined, including its elaborate glass ceiling.

The fire appeared to have started in the restaurant's dumpster near the building. A crank had been complaining about the presence of dumpsters in small, mainly residential streets like Camac, and was believed to have set others on fire before but was never arrested. In any event, Deux Cheminées was gone. As the two men stared at the smoldering remains, Gorse asked Blank if he was willing to start over. Blank didn't hesitate: Yes.

After looking at a number of properties, Blank and Gorse settled on the two late-Victorian townhouses at 1221 Locust once occupied by the Princeton Club. Much of the interior had been stripped, so the new owners went on a decorating binge, buying the mantels, carpets, drapes, paintings, and chandeliers that gave the new location its lived-in opulence. Blank was especially happy with the kitchen, which was four times larger than the former one. What's more, there were two squash courts, intact from the Princeton Club era, into which he could fit the walk-in food storage, a refrigerator, and a freezer.

The restaurant reopened about a year after the fire, welcomed by local food writers and buoyed by good notices from reviewers like Mimi Sheraton. "For a setting that is both romantic and historic," she wrote in *Time,* "it would be hard to beat Deux Cheminées. The rich cooking, nouvelle and bourgeoise, and the friendly staff add up to delightful if fairly expensive dinners. Good starters are the creamed wild mushroom soup and the *goujonettes* of Dover sole, the crisply fried ribbons of fish bedded down on greens and topped with creamy vinaigrette dressing. Green peppercorns add pungency to nicely sauteed duck breast, and the impeccably sauteed, crisp-yet-supple sweetbreads are delicious, even though their tomato-flavored sauce can be too intense."

With success came more stress. Whether or not Sheraton was right about Blank's sweetbreads sauce, the chef was having trouble with sauce of another kind. On a rare night off, he was arrested for driving under the influence after police stopped him for traveling the wrong way on a one-way street. "The cops made the jail experience as hellish as possible," he told me. "Metal beds without mattresses, a slop bucket for a toilet, the holding cell full of derelicts with shitty pants. First thing next morning, to the jailers' amazement, I was freed. Neil had contacted the mayor's brother."

Blank did not drink on the job, but after work, he would go to a bar called Woody's and down scotch and water, one after another. "I drank until I fell off my stool," he recalled. "Then someone would put me in a taxi and send me home.

"There was a young waiter at Deux Cheminées named David Cox. David was an orphan, and the restaurant had become a second home to him. I knew that he attended AA meetings. He had talked to me about the difficulty he'd had in admitting that booze was running his life. Well, one fall night, I was walking to Woody's when I began to ask myself why I was doing this. It was no longer fun. I continued on to the bar and sat in my usual spot. Without being asked, the bartender made me a scotch and water. I stared at it, then pushed it away and went home. I called David to tell him what I'd done, and he came right over. In a low-key way, he told me about his AA meetings. I started going. My hardest test came the first Thanksgiving I was sober. There was a traditional drinkfest with friends, and I thought I'd be a misfit, a pariah. But no one noticed I wasn't drinking. I found out I didn't need booze to be one of the gang. Sadly, David died of AIDS. His funeral was wrenching because much of the service, which he wrote himself, touched on how we at the restaurant had become his family."

I could imagine how to David Cox, Deux Cheminées had been a nurturing place to work. More so than most restaurants, it seemed to me, Deux Cheminées offered its employees a home as well as a job. The boss lived upstairs, after all, a prodigal nester who had enough experience of life to be a source of parental guidance to young men and women on the staff. He was the first one up in the morning and the one who turned off the lights at night. He was nearly always available to anyone needing advice and instruction. And he ran the place with a firm, deft hand. Like all good chefs, he had high standards that he urged everyone else to maintain, and though he didn't shout and throw things, he didn't hesitate to scold.

Deux Cheminées employees were served lunch and supper every workday in the staff dining room, and on holidays Blank cooked family-style feasts for them. The staff had lockers, showers, and uniform and laundry services—and it would not be stretching things too far to say that a doctor and lawyer were on call. When a staff member ran into private legal troubles, a partner who was an attorney often helped pro bono, as he did on one occasion when he went to court to defend a kitchen worker who had been arrested. And sometimes Blank, the biological scientist. practiced emergency medicine in his kitchen, like the day pastry chef Kevin Hargrove came to work with a swollen hand that bore two puncture wounds.

"What's that?" Blank asked.

"My cat bit me," Kevin said.

Blank wrote *"Pasturella multocida"* on a piece of paper and gave it to Hargrove. "Take this right away to the emergency room at Jefferson," he said, referring to the teaching hospital several blocks from the restaurant.

When Hargrove returned, he told Blank, "I gave them the paper and they said, 'Who wrote this?' I said, 'The chef where I work.' They said, 'He may have saved your life.'"

Another time, a young woman caught her arm in a meat slicer in the Deux Cheminées kitchen. The common reaction would have been to remove the arm immediately, but Blank knew she would have bled to death. Instead, he went with her to the Jefferson E.R., machine and all. She lost her arm, unfortunately, but not her life.

"I cooked Christmas dinner for the staff," Blank told me with satisfaction one winter. "Two standing ribs—they ate it all—sweet potatoes, and Kevin's bread pudding. Lights were turned down, candles lit, and so on. I ducked out to take my eighty-year-old cousin to the Academy of Music to hear the Singers perform the Messiah, and when I got back, the staff gave me an ovation. I'll cook a New Year's Eve dinner for them, too. Ham, lima bean soup, cabbage. All the farty stuff."

Several years after I first spied him in the Deux Cheminées office, Neil Gorse decided he had had enough of city life. "I'm out of here," he told me one day. Next I heard, he was traveling in Asia, and then Blank reported that Gorse had bought a house on the Gulf of Thailand where he intended to spend the better part of each year, raising orchids and enjoying the beach life. Gorse's chores at the restaurant were taken over by the maître d'. Blank was not happy to lose his friend in this way, but he seemed to adjust. He sent me a copy of emails the two men had exchanged, as he often did with friends, one January after Blank had a bout of fulminating cellulitis, a leg affliction caused by his diabetes.

"Neil: In case you haven't received the card, you will be getting a *National Geographic* renewal from me as your Christmas gift. I know, I know, you don't read it, but now that your time is less demanding, maybe you'll at least thumb through them.

"Jim [Petrie, the maître d'] and I went over the payroll raises," he explained to Gorse, who had retained his financial interest in the restaurant. Several staff got no raise (too soon from their hire date), and most everyone else got 5%. I gave 1/2 of the raise in my salary to Yvette [Knight, the prep chef]. She has really matured and has taken on a lot of responsibility. I proposed giving the other half to Jim. He declined but thanked me for the offer.

"My health has been good, and I am actually feeling rather chipper. Our longer-than-usual telephone conversation at Christmas was most uplifting, and the seasonal busy-ness and not having to work in a sweatbox ameliorates my discomfort, frustrations, and depression, and I am actually enjoying cooking again. I work while sitting at the staff dining room table and let the apprentices do the heavy schlepping and running around. (Sitting in a restaurant kitchen to work is not very professional, but my legs and feet are very grateful.) Yvette takes care of a lot of tasks that I had always assigned to myself, and overall, I feel productive again.

"I still do hope to spend less time 'downstairs' so I can get some of my cookbook compositions in presentable order. I was considering perhaps working only four days in the kitchen and one day in the library.

"Well, that's all the news that's fit to print—for now.

"Hugs, Fritz"

Gorse's reply:

"hi fcb

"thanks for the update. seems OK to me if you spend your time sitting down or in the library, whatever is best for you. just make sure that the staff knows that you are watching the quality, wherever you are. steve r____ tells me he is coming for a visit in february. that should be fun. i had hoped you would be coming too. i hope he can eat the thai food. i don't relish eating western food with him every day. well, take care and give my regards to all. Neil"

Later that year, a local food writer asked Blank to contribute to an article she was preparing on favorite meals for special occasions. This is what he told her:

"To Maria Gallagher, the *Philadelphia Inquirer*

"Hi Maria:

"Sorry I've taken so long in answering your query. Haven't had time to do anything lately but peel potatoes.

"Gee, my birthday at Deux Cheminées? Well, my birthday is in August, but I should rather like to celebrate it in December, when our menu and the holiday spirit reflect 'a few of my favorite things,' as the song goes. I would invite only one person to my party, my closest friend for over thirty years [meaning Gorse], and I would choose to be seated at number 31, my favorite table, though it's my favorite for no particular reason.

"I would start my meal with our *amuse bouche*, a small piece of quiche Lorraine, or else a two-inch piece of the Sicilian Christmas sausage I made this year. This little introduction would set the tone for the evening, and I would savor it deliberately with all my senses. For the meal proper, I would order crab soup, then perhaps some Beluga caviar or foie gras, depending on my mood and appetite of the moment. Next would be a pear salad, then rack of lamb, the cheese course, a simple not-too-sweet dessert (I am diabetic), and an espresso. Alas, I do not drink alcohol, so I would confine my beverage selection to Perrier, but would invite my dinner partner to order liberally from our wine list.

"So, that's it, my dear Maria, a birthday dinner for me by my own hand and in my own home, which is what Deux Cheminées has been for me these past twenty-plus years.

"Hugs."

11.

An Oxford Education

*B*LANK SPOKE OFTEN of the Oxford Symposium on Food and Cookery, an annual gathering of food fanciers and the occasional chef, like himself, who shared an intellectual appetite for the history, science, and culture of gastronomy. He had attended for years, first lured there by his mentor and friend Louis Szathmary, the Chicago chef and restaurateur. Because it extolled "commensality," a catchword among food scholars suggesting egalitarian fellowship, the symposium was in theory open to all, regardless of occupation or academic credentials. Even a tyro like me, who barely knew Antonin Carême from *crème brulée,* was eligible to attend. But I dithered about going. A bookish symposium seemed a distraction from learning kitchen skills. For the time and money I would spend traveling to the U.K. and back, I could take a week of cooking classes in, say, Provence or Tuscany. Besides, what could be said about fish (the year's topic was "Fish: Food from the Waters") that might not spoil after several days of classroom talk? Still, I liked the notion of gastronomes meeting in a great citadel of learning.

By the time I made up my mind to go, the symposium was fully subscribed. Blank, kind and resourceful, pulled strings for me. I took British Airways overnight from Philadelphia. At dawn, as the plane approached London, the city looked spectral and monochromatic in the early light. Peering down, I could make out familiar shapes, as in a diorama: St. Paul's, the National Gallery, St. James Park, and the curve of the Thames from Waterloo Bridge to Battersea. At Heathrow I caught a bus for Oxford and passed through countryside that echoed the vanished pastures of my youth. How could England, so much older and more densely populated than the United States, retain its agricultural lands while we rushed to pave ours over?

I took a suitably bookish garret room in a hotel not far from central Oxford. Downstairs in the dining room, the components of English breakfast languished under heat lamps: fried tomatoes, baked beans, fried eggs, sausage links, blood pudding. Blank was staying at the tonier Randolph Hotel, near the town center. I walked over there at mid-day and found him in the baronial lobby, dozing in an armchair. Though drowsy from his own red-eye flight, he was game for sightseeing. We boarded an open-air tour bus and rode through streets surging with students, residents, and tourists. Oxford was bigger and busier than I had imagined, but the hubbub did not dim the spectacle of the old spired colleges and their flawless lawns and gardens.

We got off at Magdalen College and visited the grand dining hall, which was very grand indeed. One might expect to find Sir John Gielgud there, presiding with donnish hauteur as he did in so many Oxbridge films. Next we saw the rooms Oscar Wilde once occupied, then went outside to walk in the water meadow and deer park. Returning on foot to the Randolph, we passed through the covered market, a warren of food stalls with an extraordinary variety of meat on display. Though our stomachs said it was time for a snack, we resisted the urge to eat there, saving our appetites for tea in the Randolph's vaulted dining room, where we addressed a tray of sandwiches, scones, clotted cream, and peach confit. The surroundings reminded me of the grand Green Room at the Hotel DuPont in Wilmington, Delaware, an observation I shared with Blank. "Yes, it is like the Green Room," said the chef-microbiologist, "only dirtier." (The Randolph has since been renovated.)

The symposium began the next morning at St. Antony's College, the university's postgraduate center for international studies. Into a small auditorium filed some two hundred cookery enthusiasts, many with delectable names such as Pepita Aris (noted Spanish cookbook writer), Fuchsia Dunlop (British expert on Chinese food), Astri Riddervold (leading Norwegian food academic), Cherry Ripe (Australian food writer), and Sami Zubaida (co-author of *Culinary Cultures of the Middle East*). Several in the room would be known to most American gastronomes, including Anne Willan, Alan Davidson, Harold McGee, Mimi Sheraton, Raymond Sokolov, and Jeffrey Steingarten. With evident regret, Steingarten, the food columnist for *Vogue,* put aside his cigar, half-smoked, before entering the auditorium.

The first to address the gathering was Theodore Zeldin, a founder of the symposium. The author of the five-volume *History of French Passions,* our speaker resembled, through affinity perhaps, the choleric philosopher Voltaire. Zeldin said he was pleased see so many new symposiasts among us, and he encouraged us to introduce ourselves to one another. (When I spoke to Zeldin later and received his cold shoulder in return, I gathered that he did not wish us to introduce ourselves to him.) Then Davidson came to the podium. The author of *North Atlantic Seafood, Mediterranean Seafood,* and *The Oxford Companion to Food* wore a shirt of deep magenta that set off his white hair. He began by lamenting the decline of fisheries worldwide. There was a time, he said, when 40 percent of all recipes were for cooking fish. That this was no longer true was a pity, Davidson said, because pound for pound, fish provided more nourishment (less skeleton, more muscle) than creatures of the land and air. Furthermore, he said, while it was certain that fish stocks were dwindling, there was no satisfactory way to monitor the decline because there was no common nomenclature for the world's species. Worse still, the lack of a universal nomenclature permitted the misnaming of fish for marketing purposes. The Chilean sea bass, so popular in restaurants, was not necessarily from Chile's waters and was certainly not bass. Said Davidson, "I've been shocked, though in a small way, that the Americans have taken a name out of another family for the sake of selling."

Davidson's was by no means a formal address. While he was

speaking, a member of the audience came forward and handed him a document that he received with surprise and pleasure. It was, the benefactor announced, a translation of all known medieval Arab fish recipes. Moments later, while describing his quest to formulate the proper timing for cooking fish, Davidson was interrupted again, this time by Steingarten, who was concerned about a schism in Asia over the appropriate time to kill fish. The Japanese, Steingarten said, believe that fish die the moment they are taken from their natural habitat, while the Chinese make a show of keeping fish alive in restaurant tanks. He noted that the Japanese consider those Chinese fish on display to be dead, and say their own fish are the freshest because they are killed immediately when removed from their native habitat.

Chef Blank, wearing a T-shirt promoting Spam, rose from his seat to enter the fish-killing discussion. The proper time to kill a fish, he said, might depend on the intended method of cooking. For example, some fish are best if they are steamed soon after killing, but others should be kept awhile if they are to be fried.

Harold McGee, the noted writer on food and science, proposed a fish-cooking formula he had concocted with an elder colleague, the Oxford physicist Nicholas Kurti. Contrary to the widely accepted Canadian method, which specifies ten minutes of cooking time per inch of thickness for a piece of fish, McGee and Kurti had concluded that the time needed for heat to penetrate to the center of an object varied not in simple proportion to the object's smallest dimension (usually its thickness) but rather in proportion to the square of that dimension. At McGee's direction, slips of paper were passed around the auditorium. They said: "DOUBLE THE THICKNESS OF A PIECE OF FOOD AND ITS COOKING TIME QUADRUPLES."

I was beginning to feel like a spectator at a tennis match. No sooner had McGee made his pitch for a reformulation in fish cooking than Blank was on his feet again. "What about the period of time when food continues to cook after the heat source has been removed? Have you made allowance for that?" McGee admitted he had not. Then Riddervold, a woman of formidable height and temperament, declared, by way of credentials, that she ate fish for dinner six times a week. "I cook it many ways," she said, "and one way is to put the fish in cold water and then turn on the heat. So your tables are useless."

McGee received the dissents with good humor and yielded the floor to a woman who wished to inform us that cooking time had been measured in the Middle Ages by the number of rosaries recited as heat was applied to a dish. From this had come the taboo against whistling in kitchens, for whistling was an extraneous noise that could interrupt the recitation and muck up the count. I remembered having received this same morsel of food trivia from Chef Blank.

After the introductory session, symposiasts dispersed to smaller meeting rooms. Because so many papers had been prepared and the symposium's egalitarian character allowed them all to be presented, it was necessary to hold two or three sessions simultaneously. The topics on offer at the moment concerned the fishing industry in Romansh Switzerland and the Scandinavian fish preparation called lutefisk. Blank and I chose to hear about lutefisk, a concoction made, so I learned, from dried cod. It required repeated soakings, including a two-day immersion in a solution of water and potash lye. Some adventurous eaters, notably Scandinavians, adored the gelatinous and translucent substance that resulted. Many more, I gathered, loathed lutefisk and mocked it. The fellow giving the paper, an Australian, was among the loather-mockers. He wore a white suit, perhaps in homage to the comedian Steve Martin, and worked the room for laughs. But Blank, an advocate of pickling, brining, and other forms of food conservation, was not amused. Nor was an Englishwoman in our row who indicated her displeasure with the speaker by conspicuously reading a newspaper. At the conclusion, the Norwegian Riddervold rose to her full height and declared the paper to be rubbish.

Weightier lectures followed. Joan Alcock, author of a book on Britain in Roman times, presented evidence that Romans of the second century A.D. had maintained fish farms in Cambridgeshire and Oxfordshire. She reminded us that the Roman presence in the British Isles lasted four hundred years, a span equivalent to the time from the Elizabethan era to the present. Romans used every part of the fish, she said, including heads, tails, and guts that were made into fish sauce. The final paper of the morning also dealt with sauce, and was given by an American food historian who had done a great deal of research into ketchup. The concoction Americans use on hamburgers, he said, started out as a fish sauce in China, and early renditions of it included anchovies.

That afternoon, after tea, Blank gave his paper, on parasites and farm-raised salmon, to a near-capacity crowd in the college's large common room. "I'm interested in aquaculture because the future of the world depends on the safe and effective harvesting of the sea," he said. "Modern fish husbandry actually began in the 1730s, when carp were raised from eggs to market-size. But it has taken more than two hundred years for aquaculture to become a major industry. Now, in the midst of the boom, we have to look at the consequences of raising large populations of sea creatures in confined areas. So far, the major problem marine biologists and ecologists have identified is the sea lice infestation of the Atlantic salmon. To a sea louse, aquaculture means free lunch."

Blank described sea lice as small crustaceans belonging to the order copepoda, within which more than 7,500 species have been identified. Two species of copepoda are natural parasites of salmon. The larger and more voracious of the two, *Lepeophtheirus salmonis*, can cause the host fish to sicken and die. In the mid-1990s, Blank said, fish farms in the region of Passamaquoddy Bay, New Brunswick, lost approximately 15 percent of their revenue to sea lice.

To research his paper, Blank had visited the Canadian Department of Fisheries and Oceans Biological Station in St. Andrews, New Brunswick, while visiting his friend and former maître d',

Micheline Edmunds, at her summer place in St. Andrews. While he spoke, I marveled at how he had managed to assemble his scholarly paper amid all the other demands on his time. To be sure, some of what he said that day went over my head, especially his description of chemical agents that had been used against the parasites with inconclusive results. But the scientists in the room listened intently, and at the end, they pressed him with questions. Clearly, they considered him a colleague.

The next day I heard a paper on medieval Arab fish cookery. The speaker had discovered recipes from the caliph's court in tenth-century Baghdad, and a "fish" dish that was not fish at all but a representation of a fish made from hundreds of walnuts. "I don't know why anyone would want to do that," he concluded. "What can I say? They didn't have television." Then Ken Albala, chair of the history department at the University of the Pacific and author of *Eating Right in the Renaissance,* spoke about fish phobia in the dietary theory of the European Renaissance. According to Albala, an aversion to fish and other "watery" foods, such as fruits and vegetables, extended from the mid-1400s to the mid-1600s. Animal flesh was preferred for its apparent similarity to our own bodies and ease of conversion into our own flesh. Fish, on the other hand, offered merely "thin and watery sustenance." Moreover, it was believed that because fish inhabited "cold and moist humors, [they] therefore tend to increase phlegmatic humors in the consumer." Only the lower classes, the "poor and desperate," were fit to eat fish, unlike the scholars whose wits required "the rapid movement of spirits through the brain." Stories of the ancients and their outlandish fish banquets, were, to Renaissance dietitians, sufficient evidence of the degenerative effect of fish on civilization.

Harold McGee, who followed Albala, spoke of an unforeseen consequence of overfishing the oceans: "As we exhaust our favorites, we may find ourselves mining the ocean for species we don't know too much about." At home in California not so long ago, he said, he and his wife had eaten a quantity of escolar, a deep-water fish from the South Pacific they had bought in a local market. Since they were unaware that escolar contains an indigestible wax ester that can provoke diarrhea, McGee and his wife spent several excruciating hours at a party after their escolar dinner coping with what a helpful member of the Oxford audience called a "fecal emergency."

Of his many friends among the regulars at the Oxford symposium, Chef Blank was especially fond of Nicholas Kurti, an Oxford physicist and an enthusiastic cook who, like Louis Szathmary, was a native of Hungary. Despite the fact that he was approaching his ninetieth birthday, Kurti still rode a bicycle around Oxford, sometimes pedaling over the cobbled streets to dine at his college, Brasenose. In all the years Szathmary and Blank had attended the symposium together, Kurti had never invited them to the Brasenose table, perhaps because Szathmary could be loudly critical of the food he was served. In any event, Kurti now invited Blank to supper at his college, and invited me as well.

I met Blank at the Randolph, and after a snack of quinine water and stale peanuts, we set off on foot down Magdalen Street and over to Radcliffe Square. Kurti was waiting for us at the Brasenose portal, wearing a black poncho and white bicycle helmet. Though Brasenose, founded in 1519, is not the oldest of Oxford's colleges (University College dates to 1249 or possibly, some believe, to the ninth-century reign of Alfred the Great), it still is old enough to have a central location in old Oxford, near the Bodleian and Radcliffe Camera libraries. Its odd name derives from a bronze door-knocker in the shape of a "brazen nose"—a suitable emblem for a scholar-gastronome like Kurti.

Blank and I followed him into the quadrangle, around the carpet of lawn, and into a faculty drawing room where he served sherry and showed us a food anthology he and his wife, Giana, had assembled from the writings of England's leading physicists. It was one of the most improbable books ever issued by the Royal Society's Institute of Physics, he said, but also one of the most successful. "The number of books in print about food is about the same as those on erotica," Kurti said. "This must mean that the attraction of both subjects is about equal."

We were joined in the drawing room by an executive of the Rhodes Scholarship program and an American fundraiser from New York. ("I go to lunch and dinner for a living," he said. "I'm a beggar in a suit.") Then a senior fellow of the Brasenose law faculty came in and greeted us warmly. The last to arrive was a stout Anglican clergyman dressed all in black but for the white collar below his red hair and rosy cheeks. The youngest among us, he bowed slightly and clicked his heels during introductions.

The faculty dining room was more clubby than grand. The walls were of dark wood paneling, and the white damask tablecloth, covered with silverware, crystal, and china, smelled agreeably of sachet. We took our seats, noting the wines set out for us, a white from the Loire and a red Bordeaux, then set upon the appetizer of raspberries and melon balls.

The conversation started with a low-key appraisal of Oxford food, including speculation on the best table among the thirty-odd colleges. According to the Oxonians present, students of All Souls, across Radcliffe Square from Brasenose, were particularly well fed. "Christ Church also does well," said the law professor. After a significant pause, he added, "Quite remarkable in view of a chronic lack of funds." His colleagues smiled. Christ Church, the largest college and a bastion of England's aristocracy, was anything but impoverished. As for our own fare, Blank said later that the meat, announced as veal, was closer to beef. But never mind; it had been nicely prepared and presented.

Talk moved on to Oxford customs, such as the wearing of academic gowns. I had seen few gown-wearers in Oxford and none at

Brasenose, but my companions assured me they were still around. I was told that some faculty members, fond of custom, wore their gowns to dinner at home, and if students or other dons happened to be visiting, all would parade single file into the dining room in order of academic rank. I was relieved that our Brasenose hosts were not so tied to ritual, but then they surprised me. After dessert of fruit tart and cream, when I thought the meal might be ending, we were asked to adjourn momentarily to the drawing room and carry our napkins with us. When we returned, the tablecloth had been removed and wines in decanters—a red, a white, and port— had been set out with a large plate of cheese. The senior fellow rearranged our seating, and when we had taken our new places, the electricity was turned down and we sat in candlelight.

I was now between the chaplain and the law dean. The latter told me of an American student he had once advised who hailed from the state of Georgia. Although he came from a line of Georgia lawyers and was clearly suited to the profession, he had decided not to enter practice. The problem, the young man said, was air conditioning. Before its arrival, Georgia lawyers took summers off and went to the seaside. But nowadays, they worked in the city all summer long. Air conditioning, the young man declared, had ruined the practice of law in the South.

When I turned to speak with the chaplain, I learned that he had been a public school teacher for a number of years before entering the ministry. Now he conducted two services a day at the college and tutored Greek and Latin. "It's a good congregation," he said. "Good listeners." He inquired after my religious affiliation. Many of my forbears had been Quakers, others Church of Scotland, I told him, but the family eventually became Episcopalian. The current attitude of the present Church of England, the chaplain said, had grown out of resistance to the joyless austerities of Cromwell and the Puritans. We agreed that we preferred a church that saw some virtue in pleasure. On cue, the decanters traveling around the table arrived in front of us.

"I've heard that some of the Oxford colleges have big wine collections," I said.

"That may be true for some," the chaplain said. "Brasenose has a modest cellar. I keep it, you see. I buy the wine for the college, and even have a bit of space for my own bottles." I liked the idea of a chaplain moonlighting as cellar-master.

When the cheese was nearly gone, the chaplain rose from his chair. "If you will excuse me, I have a duty to perform." He went to the sideboard, picked up a small silver box, tapped it several times, and opened the lid. Then he offered it around. The box held a red-brown powder that smelled of cedar. Over the years, in all my investigations and occasional dissipations, I had never tried snuff. With some tutoring, I placed a bit of it on the side of my hand, below the thumb, and sniffed. It was pleasantly spicy, though I have to admit that, more than the sensation of taking snuff, I enjoyed receiving it from a clergyman.

After leaving the table, the group talked a while longer in the drawing room, and then Blank and I saw Kurti into a cab. For the rest of the symposium, he was often in evidence, rising to his feet to make a point in his incisive, peppery way.

Sadly, he died several months later. A long obituary in the *Guardian* spoke of his many accomplishments in science. It also mentioned his devotion to gastronomy and quoted him as citing the words of the epicure Lord Rumford: "While we can and do measure the temperature in the atmosphere of the planet Venus, we have no real idea of what goes on inside our soufflés."

12.

Down South

"*H*ELLO. I'M JULIA CHILD. I do television and write books. I find writing very difficult, so I'm always wanting to learn more."

Sure. Julia Child, queen of all cookery, wore a lavender dress and a benign smile. She was speaking to about seventy of us who had assembled for the annual Professional Food Writers' Symposium at the Greenbrier in White Sulphur Springs, West Virginia. The four-day gathering had just started, and a microphone was being passed through the room so that everyone, including Julia, could declare their profession and purpose in coming. The dozen or so up on the dais with Julia Child had come to give talks and participate in panel discussions. Most of their names were well known in food journalism and cookbook writing: Antonia Allegra, the founder and director of the symposium; Anne Willan; Dorie Greenspan; Shirley Corriher; Lynne Rosetto Kasper; and Cara De Silva.

I was sitting next to Chef Blank, the only person there I knew except for Greenspan, a *Travel Holiday* colleague. He had attended the symposiums for years, and was known to many in the room. "I am part-owner and the chef-de-cuisine of a restaurant in Philadelphia," he said when the microphone reached him. "I am also a food historian and a food scientist, and I have a culinary library of fifteen thousand volumes. Some day when I stop peeling potatoes, I want to write my own cookbooks and put them in my own library and maybe on your shelves, too."

He had plenty of company, though not everyone in the gathering had sights set on cookbook writing. Some said they were food journalists who wanted to improve their skills or increase their readership. Others worked in the food industry and hoped to make their newsletters and press releases more readable and effective. But as the microphone made its way around, I figured that about half the attendees shared Blank's urge to write recipes for posterity.

As for my own motive in coming, I had a journalist's curiosity about recipe writers and their peculiar trade. And as a user of cookbooks, I had a burning (well, let's say simmering) question: Why do so many of us find cookbooks alluring, even addicting? Alan Davidson, editor of the *Oxford Companion to Food,* once admitted, "I tend to head for the library rather than the kitchen." I understood what he meant. I could spend so long researching an intended dish, reading the atmospheric remarks preceding the list of ingredients and directions, that I would use up most of the time available for cooking.

For example, *Cook's Illustrated,* in its magazine and cookbooks, often describes at length the trials and errors that led to the recipe it ended up publishing. It did this, I supposed, to buttress the claim that it had arrived at the perfect pot roast or ultimate lemon tart. I dutifully read those research sagas, impelled by the autonomic politeness that makes one listen patiently while a friend describes some arduous surgery or a bad encounter with airport security. Similarly, I might consult Corriher's *Cookwise* for her scientific perspective on making deviled eggs (about which she had a surprising amount to say), and end up reading the entire sixty-page chapter, "Eggs Unscrambled."

Or I might pick up *Hoppin' John's Low Country Cooking,* by John Martin Taylor, and come across this bit of amplification for Duck Breasts on the Grill: "Sunny Davis is from Walterboro, South Carolina, near the black and sinuous Ashepoo River, about an hour from Charleston. She comes from the Low Country Barnes family, one of the few who have not lost their rural traditions. The Barnes sisters—Erlene, Rena, Leslie Rae, and RuRu—are all great cooks, and their brother, Russell, is a stalwart for tradition. Whenever I have a question about real Low Country food or farming, I call a Barnes. Russell still renders his own lard in an outdoor kettle, stirring it all day with what looks like an oar but is in fact a 'lard paddle.'" And so on, and on.

In my brief life in the kitchen before I met Chef Blank, Risa and I had consulted cookbooks only on special occasions. We used the 1975 *Joy of Cooking* and, from the 1960s *Time-Life* picture book series, *The Cooking of Vienna's Empire*. Then along came Pierre Franey's memoir, *A Chef's Tale*, which made cooking seem less occult and helped impel me toward Blank's classes. Buying just one cookbook, of course, could be compared to eating a single pomme frite. Soon I bought Franey's *60-Minute Gourmet*. Then came Paula Wolfert's *Couscous and Other Good Food from Morocco* and Diana Kennedy's *The Tortilla Book*. I imagined that I had started a collection.

But then I saw Blank's library at Deux Cheminées, already huge and growing. He had discovered online shopping, and books were accumulating at such a rate that Neil Gorse had urged him to cool it. Infected by Blank's cookbook fever, I began to make purchases at the Cook Book Stall while shopping for food at the Reading Terminal Market. And at the annual Book and the Cook Fair, which drew cookbook writers to Philadelphia for a week or more of carousing and promotion, I bagged signed volumes from Corriher, Jessica Harris, and Vertamae Grosvenor, among others. Perhaps it was Harris, who wrote about the food of the African diaspora, who joked that so many cookbooks were signed by their authors that the few left unsigned might be more valuable in the end.

When traveling, I cased bookshops and museum stores for their regional cookbooks. In Juneau I bought a 1958 edition of *Out of Alaska's Kitchens*, which had recipes for Mock Ham Loaf (2 cans Spam, 1/4 pound bacon, etc.), Caribou Chunks in Gravy, and Salmon à la Newberg on Toast. I can't say I used that book much, but I did use Yvonne Ortiz's *A Taste of Puerto Rico*, which I picked up in San Juan and found helpful both in the mercado and at the stove. At Ghost Ranch in Abiquiu, New Mexico, I found a paperback called *Flora's Kitchen,* slim but expertly produced, that introduced me to the cooking of the *manitos,* the Spanish-speaking settlers of northern New Mexico. Perhaps it was a sign of fixation that while visiting Risa's cousins in Vienna, I bought a handsome volume on the bistro (*beisln*) cooking of Vienna, which featured "über 30 Rezepten." I could hardly comprehend a word of German, but no matter. Clearly, I had caught cookbook fever. When Fritz Blank talked about an annual meeting for people who actually wrote cookbooks, or had notions of doing so, I couldn't resist.

From the outset of the Greenbrier symposium, it was clear that writing a cookbook with any expectation of making money from it was no walk in the park. A panel of editors and agents described to us the Catch-22 of breaking into the business. The surest route to publication, they said, was to have successfully published before. But then they reminded us that two of the most profitable and influential cookbooks ever printed were first-time efforts. *Mastering the Art of French Cooking,* whose co-creator was in our midst, had been written with very little financial backing and was famously rejected by the first major house to contract for it. And Irma Rombauer had gambled her widow's inheritance on the first printing of *The Joy of Cooking* and sold copies door-to-door.

As it happened, Julia Child's biographer, Noel Riley Fitch, had been invited to speak at the symposium. On the afternoon of the first day, she was part of a panel that discussed alternative forms of food writing, such as biography and food history. Fitch said she had spent six years writing *Appetite for Life,* Child's authorized biography. "My work schedule was eleven to fourteen hours a day," she said. "My previous books had been in other fields, and I was new to food writing, so I immersed myself in the Food Channel as part of my research. That helped me understand Julia Child's world, though I have to admit I never figured out what Emeril Lagasse was doing."

At a reception that evening, I found Fritz Blank and Julia Child having a *tête-à-tête* in the bar. Both were drinking mineral water and had propped themselves against bar chairs to ease their gimpy legs. Blank introduced me. Child nodded and smiled at me in a familiar way, as though we shared some droll secret. She said, "I'm using a cane these days, you see. It's wonderful. I can wave it around if I want to emphasize a point or I need to get someone's attention. It's rather like carrying a sword. If I had known this, I would have started using a cane long ago." I didn't want to interrupt their chat and moved on. I knew that Blank would fill me in later on their conversation.

At supper I sat with Dorie Greenspan, Child's collaborator on *Baking With Julia,* which is now a staple of cookbook libraries. The book had already won consequential awards, yet Dorie told me she was still nursing bruises from the labor of assembling the five hundred-page work. At the beginning of the project, a skeptical editor had growled, "We've invested two million in this book, and it's all on your shoulders." Later in the project, the skeptic told Greenspan she didn't like her voice, presumably referring to Dorie's clear and energetic way of writing. But Child stood behind her co-author.

"Winning awards is the best revenge," I said. We agreed that Dorie had chosen a catchy title for her upcoming talk: "Keeping Your Voice Without Losing Your Mind."

I heard more war stories from cookbook writers. Corriher had endured eleven years of wrangling with her publisher, through changes of regime, to make sure *Cookwise* was published in the way she had originally proposed. "I look at my job as writing technical material in very simple terms," she said. "That's slow work—plus, I have a crusade against perpetuating errors in cookbooks. If I get something wrong, sure as shootin' it will get repeated in other books." Like Greenspan, Corriher was enjoying vindication. Sales of *Cookwise* were approaching a hundred thousand copies and showed no signs of flagging.

"So, what did you and Julia talk about?" I asked Blank the next morning at breakfast. We were sitting with Corriher and Jan Main, a cookbook writer from Canada.

"Oh, this and that. Pet peeves mostly. We both detest all the emphasis on presentation—you know, food stacked up on the plate or decorated with squiggles or sprigs or whatever. It's all about eye-appeal, at the expense of taste. We're losing our sense of what good food is supposed to taste like. Julia thinks we should bring back home economics courses in the schools.

"Amen," Shirley said. "The kids could learn some chemistry, physics, and biology in the process."

"I also talked to Stephanie Hersh, Julia's new assistant," Blank said. "She told me the two of them were watching television one night when Madonna came on. 'Now there's someone I'd like to meet,' Julia said. 'But I wouldn't want to shake her hand. God knows where it's been.' Another time, they were watching "Saturday Night Live" and Julia asked Stephanie if she'd seen the famous Dan Aykroyd parody of her. Stephanie hadn't, so Julia acted out Aykroyd's impersonation of *her,* right to the end when she flopped back on the couch and goes, 'And then I die!'"

Shirley looked at her watch. *"I'll* be dead if I don't get busy with the biscuits." She had agreed to make her grandmother's Touch-of-Grace Biscuits for the morning session. Toting her own mixing bowl, she led our breakfast contingent to an elevator that took us down to the bakery, on the floor below the kitchen. In this vast, well-ordered facility, some two dozen bakers and chefs turned out all the bread and pastry for the resort. "This place runs like a Swiss watch," Blank said.

Our little group did not achieve such precision with our spontaneous assembly line, but we got the job done. Shirley mixed the dough (self-rising flour, baking soda, salt, sugar, and buttermilk; to my secret delight, she had a moment of trouble doing the math in her head). Jan Main then portioned the dough out of the bowl with an ice cream scoop. With floured hands, Blank and Corriher shaped biscuits from the dough and put them in cake pans I had sprayed with nonstick oil. Then, after a touch of melted butter, into the oven they went for fifteen minutes or so. By now the front of Shirley's dark green dress was splotched with flour. The Greenbrier had given her a smock, but she was a little too ample for it to go all the way around. "If I'm not covered in flour," she said, "I'm not doing my job."

Blank dipped a pinky in some leftover buttermilk and tasted it. "The first time I had buttermilk," he said, "I was five years old and with my parents in their car when I saw a sign for gingerbread and buttermilk. I thought, *Butter*milk! I didn't know what it was, but it sounded great—liquid butter! So I screamed and yelled and carried on so much my father turned the car around and we stopped. When I tasted it, I was as embarrassed as a five-year-old can get."

When the biscuits were ready, we marched them upstairs to the Eisenhower Suite, where our symposium colleagues fell on them with gusto, slathering them with butter and jam. As I watched the biscuits disappear, I remembered Shirley's account of traveling the country, mainly on her own steam, to promote *Cookwise*. "If your book is going to sell," she told the gathering, "you have to promote it yourself. It's no good to mope when your publisher doesn't make all the phone calls and foot all the bills for you. As my sister said, 'Don't feel peed on.' My publisher paid my transportation, and I stayed with friends to save on hotel bills. And I made lots and lots and lots of biscuits."

Promoting a cookbook in person, I gathered, was more than an economic necessity. It also gave prospective readers the opportunity to meet and size up the author whose recipes they might be using. In any sort of writing, the author-reader relationship is an intimate business—even more so, it stands to reason, when the subject is food.

When the hour came for Dorie Greenspan's talk, she went at her subject with characteristic brio. "I've been asked to speak to you about voice," she said, "by which I mean the writer's personality on paper. It's how a reader comes to know you. All the best food writing has it. Read Julia's books or Maida Heatter's or Barbara Kafka's —they all have a distinctive voice. Of course, all of you writers have a voice, too, but you might not be as confident in it as you could be, or you might not be using it to full advantage.

"Someone asked me yesterday if I had created my voice, and I said no. My voice—that reassuring, I'm-your-friend-in-the-kitchen voice—came very naturally to me. Friends would read my stuff and say, 'You know, it sounds like you.' But I never felt like enough of a writer to think, let alone say, that I had a voice. M.F.K. Fisher had a voice. Laurie Colwin had a voice. Calvin Trillin—you would know his work even if it didn't have his name on it. Secretly, deep down inside, I had to believe I had a voice because there's no other way to explain why I would tinker with my writing, over and over, and read it out loud. I'd be ready to mail the piece, and I'd grab it back and I'd change it again.

"Strangely, it was only when an editor told me she *didn't* like my voice that I was forced to admit that I had one. I was working on *Baking With Julia* at the time, and I wanted to kill the woman. Fortunately, a friend who had been reading the manuscript phoned me that same day. 'Dorie,' she said, 'I just love your voice.' I wrote the rest of *Baking With Julia* thinking about her. All of us need a cheerleader like that, someone who likes our work and we can practice on. In fact, one way to develop a voice, test out a voice, is to have someone in mind when we write. My friend Mary writes business pieces for a general audience, which requires a voice that's clear and non-technical. So Mary writes to her mother, who can't balance a checkbook.

"Now, where does voice come in when you're writing a cookbook? There's always a place for your voice in the head-notes—you know, the material that introduces the recipe. You can really have some fun here, but it's tricky because your first job is to provide information. You have to tell people about the ingredients you're asking them to buy and prepare. You have to make it sound appealing while being honest about how hard it's going to be. You can say, 'My aunt Sally made these mashed potatoes every Friday night when we came for dinner. My family loved them, and yours will, too.' We've all read head-notes like that. But that's not very helpful to the reader.

"An even-greater challenge is making the recipes come alive. When I write a recipe, I have a picture in my head of the home cook in the kitchen, and I imagine him or her going through all the steps of the recipe. When I'm developing and testing recipes, I take extensive notes. I look at the recipe at every stage, its temperature, its appearance, its texture. I taste it, of course, and I jot down potential problems so I can help the cook avoid them. I happen to write very long recipes, in part so I can include little asides.

"For example, in my instructions for kneading dough for scones, which is kind of a delicate business, I might say, be careful, don't over-knead the dough. Knead it ten times and then *stop,* even though the urge to go on will be irresistible. I talk to my readers. I say, don't worry if your crust cracks in the oven; you can always patch it. Or for cutting croissants, give up, give up! You'll never get the end pieces to look as good as the rest of the batch. But they'll make great nibbles for the baker. Anticipating your readers' problems not only makes a better recipe, it also makes it more fun to write. And you've *got* to have fun. You're writing hundreds of recipes, so you've got to amuse yourself while you're doing it."

Clearly, writing cookbooks was a good deal more difficult than I had imagined. With a twinge of shame, I also recognized that, as much as I enjoyed using cookbooks, I had looked on them as a lesser form of writing. Soon after the Greenbrier conference, while reading the memoir of Richard Olney, the expatriate artist, gastronome, and cookbook maker, I came across a sentiment Julia Child had expressed to him back in 1973: "Nobody ever thinks, as I was just writing Elizabeth David, that our kind of writing is even worth serious consideration—but it seems to me ours is much the most difficult of all. Not only must it be original, literate, and stylish, it must be fully researched and accurate. *Eh bien.*"

Soon after Greenbriar, inspired by the good times in White Sulphur Springs (to say nothing of the hominy grits, corned beef hash, chicken pot pie, and pork cooked with sauerkraut), Blank and I ventured farther south, down to the Southern Foodways Symposium in Oxford, Mississippi. We flew to Memphis and rented a car, stopping first at Jim Neely's Interstate Bar-B-Que for chopped pork shoulder, baked beans, and potato salad. Neely came out of the kitchen to inspect the out-of-towners who were devouring his food. It turned out he knew Tony Luke, the prince of roast pork in South Philadelphia. Then we drove down to Oxford, taking a country highway past towns with names reassuring to nervous Yankees: Olive Branch, Holly Springs, Bethlehem, Laws Hill.

Next morning we sidled into a booth at Smitty's, by the main square in Oxford, and scanned the breakfast menu of "biskits," "aigs," "omlets," and other artfully misspelled fare. I chose sausages, grits, and biscuits with sorghum molasses. Blank had country ham with sawmill gravy. At a table nearby, two local men in crisp cotton shirts and khaki trousers were discussing a matter of apparent gravity. I listened in and soon was sorry. They were rehashing a recent automobile accident in detail, giving particular attention to the victims' gruesome injuries. Fortunately, they spoke a chiming drawl that eased my discomfort; by tuning them out just a bit, I could imagine they were discussing crops and fishing.

The symposium, held at the University of Mississippi, was modeled to some degree on its English antecedent, the Oxford Symposium on Food and Cookery. From near and far, Tupelo and Clarksdale to Beverly Hills and Barcelona, scholars, journalists, cooks, and freelance gastronomes met for two and a half days in a handsome old hall on the Ole Miss campus for lectures, papers, and panel discussions, interspersed with brunches, lunches, picnics, wine tastings, cocktail receptions, buffets, banquets, dessert tastings, tavern crawls, and coffee breaks. One speaker, the writer John Egerton of Nashville, put it this way: "Food people get together for all the right reasons—to eat, to talk about eating, and to plan the next time to get together."

"What is the South?" asked Charles Reagan Wilson, professor of Southern studies at the university. "There are many Souths, including pockets of Southern culture in the cities of the North." Jessica Harris agreed. Her grandmother, she said, grew her own peanuts and greens in Jamaica, Queens. "Today, trucks bring Down South produce to Up South patrons." One of the principal speakers, Harris discussed "the shared lives and shared cooking styles" of blacks and whites in the Old South. William Woys Weaver and Hoppin' John Taylor grappled with the difficulty of defining Southern cuisine. There are many Southern cultures with their own styles of cooking, Weaver said; it is pointless to try to force together that which should remain regionally distinct. The American South occupies more than a million square miles, Taylor noted, which makes it larger than Western Europe. His region alone, the ten thousand square miles of South Carolina low country, had a greater variety of plants than Eastern and Western Europe together.

Taylor spoke early on Saturday, when more than a few of the hundred or so conferees were feeling the effects of Friday night's tavern crawl in Oxford Square. But no one dozed. "When I first started to study food history fifteen years ago," he said, "the field was nearly nonexistent. Why? Because cooking was women's work and therefore considered unimportant. Misogyny was just as bad in the inner circles of the food world as in other endeavors. But so much interesting material is emerging that I see culinary history getting equal emphasis with political and military history. This subject is huge."

Taylor might have added that culinary history had been slighted as well because, in the South and elsewhere, cooking was also the work of blacks. On that score, some progress was evident. Nearly half the speakers, including Professor Harris, were of African descent. Ed Scott of Drew, Mississippi, told about his career as the first African-American catfish farmer in the Mississippi Delta. Lawrence Craig of De Valls Bluff, Arkansas, talked of the barbecue business he had operated for more than fifty years. Bill Wiggins, professor of Afro-American studies and folklore at the University of Indiana, discussed a weighty subject—the role of food in the

African-American religious experience—to which he gave a frothy title: "Chickens Must Die So That Men Might Live." When he grew up in the '40s and '50s, Wiggins said, Protestant churches were the core of black communities. "If you met a black and he wasn't Baptist or Methodist, you knew someone was messin' with him." And food was always in abundance at important family and church events such as weddings, baptisms, and wakes. Even the dinner served when a young man met his intended's family was a significant ritual.

After Wiggins spoke on Sunday morning, we repaired to a dining room for duck hash, salad, and biscuits. We were full up even before the lemon blueberry pound cake was served, but then the University of Mississippi Gospel Choir, fifteen young black students, women and men, filed into the room and arranged themselves before us. As they sang the first of a dozen pieces, I thought back to my childhood, when I would be taken to hear spirituals at St. Paul's Baptist Church in West Chester, Pennsylvania. The music had swooped and shimmered. In the pews in front of me, heads bobbed, bodies rocked, hands clapped, and all the while, the smells of supper—baked chicken, biscuits, brown gravy, sweet potatoes, fresh peas—rose from the community room down in the basement. The choir sang of going up to Heaven, but surely the singers had the direction wrong. Heaven was just under our feet.

The program of the Southern Foodways Symposium mixed scholarly talks with off-the cuff observations and reminiscences—what could be called oral history. My favorite in the second category was a forty-five-minute riff and homily by Leah Chase, proprietor of Dooky Chase's in New Orleans.

"My family tree's all termite-eaten," she said by way of introduction. "Anyway, I don't worry too much about the past because I'm too busy getting where I'm going. When I got into the restaurant business in the 1940s—my husband's parents started Dooky Chase's—I had never even been inside a restaurant. There were no black restaurants in those days; away from home, blacks ate sandwiches.

"Now, about Southern cooking, I'm sorry. In New Orleans we're not Southerners, we're Creole. Whatever you are, your food should express it. You have to make the food you cook your own. So don't be bashful, get your food out where everyone can see it. People come to my restaurant to have what I make, because they know I put myself into it." She looked around the room. "Is everyone a camel? Some of you walk around with water all the time. Never mind. Now, Thanksgiving is coming up. You want to know about Creole Thanksgiving? We eat gumbo at noon, then get away from the table and have drinks. Then we go back to the table for ham, turkey, and so on."

Blank told me he had eaten at Dooky Chase's. "The food was wonderful. The meal lasted six hours." As I had expected, he was well received at the symposium. During the talks and lectures, he was not bashful about chiming in about this or that, and at mealtimes, a cluster of friends and would-be friends often gathered around him—what Betty Fussell called "FOFs," friends of Fritz." So I was not surprised when John T. Edge, the principal organizer of the symposium, invited Blank to be part of a "gumbo cookoff" at the next year's event. To our certain pleasure, Edge had declared Philadelphia to be the nation's "northernmost Creole city," because of its culinary ties to the American South and the Caribbean.

Blank emailed his acceptance to Edge: "What you call gumbo, we call Philadelphia pepper pot. Surviving recipes call for tripe as a key ingredient, but researchers now believe that tripe was a replacement for turtle after turtle meat became scarce. Not too long ago, the common belief was that Philadelphia pepper pot was invented by George Washington's cook while encamped at Valley Forge. Thanks to historians like Will Weaver and Jessica Harris, it is clear now that North American pepper pots and their kissin' cousins, gumbos, can be traced to a common origin in West Africa, with an infusion of Caribbean spice along the way.

"The pepper pot I make is thickened with pumpkin (Will Weaver's idea, which I readily embraced). I also use turtle meat (snapping) and lots of shellfish, spaetzle for dumplings, and habanero chiles for the "pepper" in pepper pot. (Even though Mark Miller of Coyote Cafe in Santa Fe thinks he invented habaneros in the 1990s, they were indeed available and used in early colonial America."

I did not go south the next year for the Leah Chase-Fritz Blank cookoff but read about it on the first page of the *New York Times* food section. The writers, Matt Lee and Ted Lee, were enthralled. "In a leafy grove," they said, "competitors ladled out their finest gumbo to 120 restaurant critics, chefs, culinary historians, and plain old eaters, who voted by applause. Leah Chase served a superb traditional Creole gumbo, a rich, smoky gravy full of good things: shrimp, chicken wings, crab legs, sausage, hunks of beef brisket. Fritz Blank ladled out a tribute to his city's pepper pot, a gumbo with all the fundamentals of Ms. Chase's: a thick soup with gentle spice and heat, textured by a variety of meats. But where Ms. Chase's soup was a brackish, silky broth thickened with roux and filé powder, Mr. Blank's was jack-o'lantern orange and velvety, thickened by a puree of rice, leeks, and butternut squash. Ms. Chase's gumbo got its pep from paprika and hot sausage, Mr. Blank's from ginger and habanero chile. Both gumbos were deeply complex, wildly exotic, and perfectly balanced all at once: alternatingly briny, hot, savory, and sweet elements mingled to mesmerizing effect, producing a slightly mysterious, almost spiritual pull that made us reach for spoonful after spoonful."

The Lees did not say which gumbo received the most applause, nor did I ask Blank about it. As they put it, the two gumbos were "so wildly different that the mere suggestion of competition seemed downright unsportsmanlike."

Leah Chase told the Lees about a gumbo she and a friend had prepared during World War II for a group of Tuskegee Airmen, the pioneering black pilots. One of the fliers was certain that the filé powder the cooks had used (a flavoring and thickening agent made by grinding dried sassafras leaves) was a voodoo potion. "Don't eat the gumbo!" he told his mates. "If you eat that gumbo, you'll never leave New Orleans."

Roquette Science

13.

*V*ALENTINE'S DAY was approaching. Blank did not like the occasion, even though Deux Cheminées was always filled, thanks to surveys listing it among the most romantic restaurant settings in town. It wasn't that he lacked a tender side. It was just that serving dinner to a house full of mooning couples involved extra expense and bother. Tables that normally held four diners or more had to be converted to two-tops, as he called them, and two-tops were a headache to serve. Moreover, many Valentine celebrants were neophytes out for a splurge, unschooled in palette and restaurant protocol. At best, they required tutoring by the wait staff. At worst, their no-show rate was high, they tipped poorly, and some thought it was cool to send back the wine.

So Blank welcomed the diversion of a mid-February visit from Harold McGee, his friend and colleague from the Oxford Symposium and the fledgling fraternity of food scientists. McGee, who lived in Palo Alto, had been invited to address the annual meeting of the American Academy for the Advancement of Science, convening that year in Philadelphia. Blank put him up in the restaurant's third-floor apartment. Because he would be speaking on the eve of Valentine's Day, McGee chose as his topic "The Death and Transfiguration of the Cocoa Bean." Blank had planned to accompany him, but when something at the restaurant went into the weeds, he asked me to show McGee around.

After breakfast I walked Blank's guest the half-dozen blocks from Deux Cheminées to the Convention Center. McGee was one of the few food enthusiasts I had encountered, beside my wife and the hyperkinetic cookbook writer Eileen Yin-Fei Lo, who might not wish to lose weight. I wanted to ask him his secret for staying slim but was afraid he might use the word "discipline." When we arrived at the venue, we learned that President Clinton would address the convention in the main hall at noon, so the morning programs would be shortened accordingly.

A representative of the AAAS introduced McGee and the other speakers. "Our subject is chocolate," he said, "but not only because of Valentine's Day. We also considered geography. When conventions are held in California, we're likely to talk about wine. Here in Pennsylvania, we're in the state that manufactures more chocolate candy, by far, than any other. And Philadelphia is close to two of the world's major chocolate producers, Hershey and Mars." He then introduced McGee, mentioning his B.S. from Cal Tech, his Ph.D. in English from Yale, and his two praiseworthy books, *On Food and Cooking* and *The Curious Cook*. As McGee got ready to speak, I looked around the meeting room. Despite the morning hour, nearly every chair was taken. The crowd seemed happy and eager, though I couldn't tell if they were keen to hear about chocolate or anticipating the samples brought by envoys from Hershey and Mars.

"The ordeal of the cocoa bean, on its way to becoming chocolate, makes a sordid story," McGee said. "Ghastly as it is, it's a story that helps us become more discriminating chocolate tasters. It begins, as many here know, with the cocoa tree, *Theobroma cacao*, which is generally found within twenty degrees of the equator. That would include, in this hemisphere, the Caribbean and Central America south to Peru and Brazil. The cocoa tree grows pods six to ten inches long and three or four inches in diameter. Inside the pod a juicy pulp surrounds a cluster of twenty to forty beans, each about an inch long. When the pods are harvested, the beans and pulp are typically removed from the pod and set out in the sun where something remarkable and gruesome happens. Microbes in the pulp—bacteria, yeast, and molds—multiply and kill the seed embryos within the beans. There's other mayhem, too: Cell walls in the beans break down, various substances combine, and bitter, astringent compounds bind and soften. This fermentation process takes a few days, and then the beans are cleaned of pulp and ready to be roasted.

"I tried fermenting beans myself in my kitchen at home. After several days in the pulp, they smelled like beer and then like vinegar. The bean is literally poisoned by the vinegar. It's sad but necessary. Without death by fermentation, the bean would not amount to much. It would not take on the thousands of complex molecules resulting in a huge variety of flavors. When I roasted unfermented beans at home, they came out horribly bland, like old dried-out black beans. On the other hand, chemical analysis of fermented and roasted cocoa beans reveals the same compounds that give taste and aroma to everything from fruits and flowers to wines, nuts, spices, and even butter and cheese.

"You might like to know that Valentine's Day also went through a dramatic transformation. It started in ancient Rome as the festival of Lupercalia, held on February 15. Young men dressed in animal skins ran around the city, slapping young women with strips of goat skin. This was supposed to ensure fertility and ward off evil. Go figure."

When the program ended and we had eaten the Mars and Hershey specimens in the name of science, McGee and I made our way to an enormous room where the president would speak. No chocolate was on offer here, but still the anticipation was palpable. Clinton was popular in the scientific community for his administration's support of research. When he appeared, radiant with celebrity, a thousand scientists stood and applauded. He congratulated the academy on its 150th anniversary. "Fifty years ago," he said, "when President Truman spoke at your 100th anniversary, the computer had just been developed, not far from here. Where do you suppose we will be fifty years from now, at the 200th anniversary? Will we have found a way to supply human needs without depleting the planet? Or will life be, as Hobbes put it, nasty, brutish, and short? We must never be afraid of the future, but we must envision the future we want."

The president went on in this vein for some time, then left, to more standing applause, to have lunch with his food buddy, Mayor Ed Rendell, at Big George's Stop-N-Dine, a Southern-style cafeteria in West Philadelphia. The two had macaroni, rice, fried chicken, and barbecue. McGee and I went to West Philadelphia, too, but only as far as the Monell Chemical Senses Center close by the Penn campus and Drexel University. Chef Blank had arranged a tour with Monell's director, Gary Beauchamp.

Otherwise indistinguishable on a block of workaday architecture, the Monell Center could be identified by the large sculpture of a nose and mouth that stood out front. The sculpture made me think of the "brazen nose" of Brasenose College, Oxford.

"The nose is our landmark and logo," Beauchamp said. "We got it through a city arts program. Maybe a dozen artists submitted proposals, and our faculty voted. The nose didn't get a single vote, but the official writing the check for the city insisted on it, and her choice turned out to be the right one."

Beauchamp led us to the top floor, from where we slowly made our way back down, past laboratories and offices. "We started out in 1968 in an old warehouse," he said. "Now we're up to sixty thousand square feet. We have about two-dozen staff members and fifteen post-doctoral fellows. What's unusual, I think, is the range of scientific disciplines represented here. I'm a behavioral biologist, and when I first arrived in 1971, I shared an office with an anthropologist and a zoologist. And I did my first research with a chemist.

"Our aim is to advance knowledge of what the chemical senses are and how they work, and, of course, to get our findings out to the academies and industries and the public. For instance, we're looking into how chemical senses play a role in food cravings. We know that many cravings are triggered by chemosensory stimulation—the smell of coffee brewing or cookies baking. But not everyone is affected equally. People with better olefaction—a more acute nose, you might say—appear to experience more-frequent cravings.

"The elderly, who often have reduced olfactory function, tend to report fewer cravings than young adults. They don't mind a monotonous diet the way young adults do. In fact, a monotonous diet actually increases food cravings in young adults, whereas the elderly are generally unaffected by a boring diet. The result could be a reduction in the variety of foods the elderly select, which may compromise their nutrition. Most studies of eating and drinking behavior concentrate on children and young adults. We're trying to remedy that because the elderly population is growing so fast."

I said, "Hal talked this morning about the fermenting process that gives the cocoa bean its complexity of flavors. Are you saying that complexity is nature's way of enticing us to eat?"

"It is certainly one of them," Beauchamp said. "People appear to like complex flavors, as well as foods in which mouth-feel, as we call it, changes over time. In addition to the taste of chocolate candy—sweet, perhaps a hint of bitter and all the rest—there is also the mouth-feel imparted by fat. When chocolate candy is in the mouth, it changes from a solid to a smooth paste because cocoa butter melts at body temperature."

McGee said, "I think most cooks learn, by trial and error, how to create flavor and texture. It usually comes down to salt and fat, the salt that brings out the taste and, say, the butter you add at the last minute to your pan sauce."

"Yes, but Americans have the tendency to overdo it," Beauchamp said. "Our studies indicate that you can reduce the salt and fat in your diet, and in a fairly short time, your taste buds won't know the difference. Reduced intake leads to reduced craving."

We came to a room of fish tanks. "Fish have many more taste receptors than humans do," Beauchamp said, "so we can run tests with them. The catfish, in effect, is almost all tongue. That's why it can detect food even at the bottom of a muddy pond. A single catfish has more receptors than all the humans in this building put together."

Before we left Monell, McGee told Beauchamp of the biennial food scientists' gathering in Erice, Sicily, known formally as the International Workshop on Molecular and Physical Gastronomy.

"It was started in 1992 by Nicholas Kurti, a physicist at Oxford," McGee said. "I thought you should know about it because the topic at the next meeting will be flavor."

"How can I resist?" Beauchamp said.

Blank had been to all but one of the Erice meetings. He, too, urged Beauchamp to attend. So it was that Gary Beauchamp found himself in a former monastery some twenty-five hundred feet above the bay of Castellamare del Golfo, in company with Fritz Blank, Harold McGee, and a swarm of scientists, including two Nobel laureates. Beauchamp was having a true busman's holiday, sampling freshly pressed olive oil from the trees of the Italian physicists Ugo Palma and his wife, Beatrice Palma-Vittorelli.

Beauchamp noted the velvety texture and fruity aroma of the Palmas' oil. Then, as he swallowed, a pronounced peppery effect contracted his throat and made him cough. He recognized the irritation. It was the same response he had experienced back at Monell when tasting liquid ibuprofen, an anti-inflammatory agent. That was the beginning of a three-year study Beauchamp and his Monell colleagues conducted into the possible anti-inflammatory properties in olive oil. The findings were published in the September 1, 2005 issue of *Nature*. The article identified a phenol compound called oleocanthal in newly pressed olive oils that "has a potency and profile strikingly similar to that of ibuprofen." Although structurally dissimilar, the article said, both molecules inhibit the same inflammatory pathway.

Blank brought some of the Palmas' olive oil home from Erice and shared it with us in the cooking class. The Erice conference, he said, had been mind-boggling. One of the Nobel Prize winners, physicist Pierre-Gilles de Gennes, had been most kind and attentive to Blank, and so had his wife, Anne-Marie de Gennes, who ran the Le Boudin Sauvage restaurant on the outskirts of Paris.

"Pierre-Gilles is an incredible intellect," Blank said, "a practical philosopher as well as a physicist. He and Anne-Marie want me to visit the restaurant. They were adamant. I don't know how I'll find time, much less figure out what I can talk about with them."

"I've never seen you at a loss for words," I said.

"Yeah, well. I had a great time with the Palmas, Ugo and Beatrice. After the conference they took me to their country house in the hills, about two hours from Palermo. No electricity, a small well, a picnic table made of granite. They produce their own wine. They make tomato sauce in a big vat over an outdoor oven. Beatrice cooks with fennel and *bourrage* she picks on the grounds. They've got eighteen cows, plus sheep and goats. I watched local shepherds make ricotta and pecorino in what I would call primitive conditions—no washing hands or udders, as far as I could tell. The Italian government is cracking down on these small rural producers, and I'm afraid they'll end up driving them out of business.

"Ugo and Beatrice have done a lot for the Erice conference. Back when Dr. Kurti was looking for a meeting site, he called Ugo. There was a scientific conference already in place in Erice, specializing in physics and cosmology, and Ugo helped secure the venue. Only later did he find out that the conference was not about astronomy but gastronomy."

After Kurti's death, the Erice gatherings went into decline. A French scientist tried to run it but did not have Kurti's grace with colleagues, and was mistrusted by some of them. Indeed, when Blank returned from the Erice meeting of 2001, he told me the Frenchman had appropriated his research material and presented it as his own.

Plagiarism wasn't the only Erice occurrence to ruffle Blank's feathers. An article about the conference that appeared in *Gourmet* prompted him to reaffirm his credentials, writing this letter to the organizer:

"Dear H___:

"I have just read 'The Gastronauts,' by Daniel Zwerdling, in the October *Gourmet,* which details a very small part of the Erice proceedings. It seems more like a PR piece for Heston Blumenthal [a science-oriented English chef] and Harold McGee, rather than a report on the purpose, scope, and activities of the N. Kurti Gastronomy Meetings at Erice. I love both Heston and Harold, but Zwerdling's essay is very much skewed.

"On a personal note, I take great offense at being called 'a 300-pound restaurateur from Philadelphia . . . his arms a mass of tattoos.' I have one tattoo on one of my arms, and I weigh considerably less than 300. I am a chef who cooks; I am not a restaurateur. Also, he implies that none of the chefs at the conference had any background in science. Is not Shirley Corriher a chemist and an accomplished cook and teacher? Do not my degrees and training in animal husbandry and medical microbiology count as a scientific background? Someone should remind Zwerdling—and we should all remember—that a kitchen is in fact a laboratory, and the equipment and methods we cooks and chefs use are as scientific as any found in any university science laboratory.

"Also, our recipes are as valid as any formula found in any pharmacopoeia. We measure volumetrically, we weigh gravimetrically, we assign degrees of specific gravity (degrees Baumé), and we measure heat and temperature using a variety of scales. We employ a huge repertoire of equipment. We cook in pots and pans—containers no less bona fide than the crucibles and flasks found in any laboratory. We use steam generators, dry heat ovens, refrigerators and freezers, electric blenders, and temperature-controlled water baths. We employ and direct microorganisms to work their biochemistry on substrates. We titrate endpoints by tasting. We use acids; we use bases; we use salts, and we stop and start reactions as needed. The entire specialty of sugar and candy cookery is based upon pure chemistry. Just like all scientists, we draw conclusions after our work, be it experimental or a standardized procedure, by using all five of our senses. We also pay careful attention to the ongoing statistical analysis of our findings by listening to the comments made by those who sample and judge the products of our labors.

"So why must an egg be cooked in a glass beaker in order to be recognized as a scientific work? Why must a cook not be considered a scientist just because he or she doesn't have liquid nitrogen and an optical refractometer in the kitchen? I am a cook. I am a scientist. I am an artist. I am a tradesman. I use my scientific training both as a husbandman and as a medical microbiologist to help me practice my art and profession as a chef who cooks good things to eat. I am able to cook by knowing and understanding science, and because of this, I am better able to produce meals for my customers to enjoy.

"I hope that all of my colleagues who attend our wonderful conferences at Erice—be they experts in the physics of crystallography, thermonuclear chemists, microbiochemists expert in the exchange of energy during yeast fermentation, molecular engineers studying the diffusion of sugars through a semipermeable membrane, physiologists who study the neuropathways of how humans perceive taste, or be they just cooks—that all are able to appreciate, as I do, the real value of our meetings, and that is that we come together in order to share our knowledge, and that the exchange is mutually beneficial."

Alas, there have been no subsequent meetings at Erice, or elsewhere, of the International Workshop on Molecular and Physical Gastronomy, though some of the conferees dream of reviving it.

Critics

$\mathcal{F}$OR SOMEONE whose livelihood required the approbation of critics, Chef Blank was generally relaxed about his treatment in the press. He did not have a publicist, unlike most of his colleagues at high-end restaurants. If he wanted to address the media, he would pick up the phone himself. Or if he felt a critic had unfairly maligned the restaurant, he might ask Neil Gorse to write an astringent reprimand.

Of course, Blank read his reviews. Soon after I started attending his classes, the *Inquirer*'s Eileen Tate wrote what seemed to me to be an eccentric appraisal of Deux Cheminées. She praised most of the meal, including an "outstanding" crab soup and "perfectly sautéed" striped bass but objected to some "limp" pastry and "supersalty" risotto that came, so she said, with shrimp that smelled past its prime. Had she raised those complaints with the staff so she could evaluate the response and allow the establishment to redeem itself? No. Blank seemed philosophical. "Eileen's just an odd duck and always has been," he said. "She once got on Peter von Starck's case about being served something at La Panetière on a chipped plate, so at a party celebrating Georges Perrier's move to new quarters, which Eileen attended, von Starck gave a flowery speech and presented Perrier with a badly chipped plate as a charm against bad reviews from Eileen. The crowd roared and Eileen squirmed."

Not long after she wrote her final review of Deux Cheminées, a restaurant she had put on the map nearly twenty years before, Tait retired from the *Inquirer*. Who would succeed her? If it had been up to me, I would have tried to lure away the restaurant critic at the

New York Observer. I had been reading the weekly for some time to follow the career of Nick Paumgarten, Risa's nephew, who later became a staff writer for the *New Yorker*. One day my eye fell on a column titled, "Dining Out with Moira Hodgson." It began this way:

"The first time I ate an American hot dog was in Vietnam. I lived in Saigon for a couple of years as a child, at a time when the increasing U.S. presence was made felt by, among other things, American snack bars that mushroomed all over town. My favorite was called, oddly, La Bodega and, besides hot dogs, it sold Coca-Cola (which I wasn't allowed at home) and played out-of-date records by Elvis Presley and Pat Boone. It had no counter, but it did have Formica tables, each of which was set with two large plastic bottles, one red and the other brown."

Was this a memoir? A food essay? A review? Hard to tell, but I read on:

"I remembered all this the other night as I found myself sitting in Mekong [a Vietnamese restaurant in SoHo] with my young son, who is about the age I was in Saigon. Our table was not Formica but set with a white paper cloth and two large, plastic squeeze bottles, one red and the other brown. These bottles did not contain mustard or ketchup, however: One was a fiery chili concoction, and the other was hoisin sauce. My son was not eating hot dogs, either, but contemplating a large bowl of *pho*, a Vietnamese beef broth made with slices of beef and noodles, which he seasoned, rather gingerly, with the sauces from the two bottles."

Was that bowl of *pho* any good? Moira Hodgson wasn't saying, at least not yet. She wrote of her arrival in New York from England in the 1960s ("the Beatles were at the top of the charts"); the proliferation of Vietnamese restaurants in New York and their types, chic and trendy on the one hand and "the Chinatown kind"—Formica tables, neon lights—on the other; Mekong's location (on the edge of Little Italy); and decor: candlelit tables, potted plants, wood floor, bamboo curtains, a long bar in the front (where a Yankees game was on TV), and a big picture of the Mekong River at sunset.

In clumsier hands, this kind of scene-setting could stultify, but reading Hodgson was so agreeable I was unaware that half her column had sped by before the food came under scrutiny. "Shrimp arrived hot and sizzling with a dipping sauce of *nuoc mam*," she wrote. "Whole red snapper was barbecued and topped with lemongrass and a complex green pepper sauce, which brought out the flavor of the very fresh fish. Peppery beef saté was served on what looked like a little bathmat, made of steamed vermicelli noodles, as was the grilled lemongrass pork, topped with scallions and roasted peanuts. Fried calamari was excellent, too, spicy and crisp, flavored with ginger and onion." At end of the meal, "We walked home humming the tunes from the Beatles songs we had listened to all evening." She gave Mekong two stars.

The next Hodgson review I saw dealt with a chic new spot in Tribeca where "the calimari were a bit chewy and the äioli could have had more garlic. As I worked on the squid, we discussed the new movie "Portrait of a Lady," and I thought of Henry James, who used to 'fletcherize' his food, chewing every mouthful thirty times. Violet Hunt, a writer spending the weekend at his house, was feeling very ill one morning after eating a spoiled lobster bisque the previous night, but she had to sit in front of James at breakfast and watch him fletcherize his cereal, which was topped with a fried egg." On her second visit to this restaurant, Hodgson and her party had to settle for a table by the front door. "I dug into a satisfying warm chicory salad tossed with lardons of bacon, roasted shallots, and crumbled blue cheese," she said. "A large roast portobello mushroom with Swiss chard, arugula, and creamy white beans was good, too, like a steak. My husband had ordered what was listed on the menu as 'Greek' salad with feta and oregano, which in ironic quotes or not turned out to be perfectly respectable. As he was eating it, a man passed by and slapped my husband in the face with his coat, then walked on, oblivious. 'I apologize for him to you,' whispered the waitress. As she bent over the table to refill my husband's wine glass, another man walking past pinched her behind and she gave a yelp. 'I apologize for him to you,' said my husband. She burst out laughing."

What more could I wish for? Moira Hodgson gave me the vicarious experience of eating out in New York while sparing me the expense and inconvenience of going there. Over time I came to feel that, in a harmless and distant way, I knew her and her family, as well as her reliably droll friends. They often seemed to be performing vignettes in Woody Allen movies. "How is it?" she asked a companion who had ordered ostrich at an East Village bistro. "It tastes like horsemeat with wings," he said. At an intimate spot on West Broadway, Hodgson drew a table close to a couple drinking Dom Perignon: "The man handed his date the cork and she slipped it into her handbag. 'I'll pay you to live with me,' he said, naming an exorbitant monthly sum. 'And even if you decide to leave, I'll still take care of your mother.'" Once, at Hodgson's own table, a woman companion was applying herself to some overcooked swordfish when "an attractive young man in a blue Nehru jacket came over and said, 'I just had to tell you, you are incredibly beautiful.' Later, as we were winding up dinner with ginger cheesecake and crème caramel, the man in the Nehru jacket returned. He took my friend by the hand and looked her in the eye. 'I would like to continue this,' he said. 'Thanks, but I'm married and I have seven children,' she replied. He jumped up as though he had been shot, and disappeared without another word."

Not only did I get vicarious enjoyment from Hodgson's restaurant escapades, I also found myself agreeing with her tastes and views. She liked, among other things, salt cod, sweetbreads, the plaintive Portuguese ballads called fado, foie gras, Argentine tango, caviar, Moroccan food and *dulce de leche*. I liked all those, too. We disliked, in common, salad bars ("when you've been around the table once," she wrote, "you realize you don't want to eat anything on it at all"), cigar smoke, most background music, restaurants that won't seat you until "your party is complete," food plated vertically ("like teased hairdos"), waiters who ask, "Are you still working on that?" and "piss-elegant" menu jargon like *amuse-gueule* and *amuse-bouche*.

Above all, I liked Hodgson's way of putting things. "His pea soup was a vivid deep green, laced with wild mushrooms," she wrote. "It tasted the way peas do when you pick them off the vine on a warm day and eat them standing in the garden." And, "Feeling reckless, I ordered roasted marrow bones. They looked like monolithic sculptures placed around an unmown lawn." And, "The asparagus soup . . . is a light, airy concoction, giving . . . a pronounced taste of asparagus complemented by the faint but persistent aroma of Parmesan that comes through like a voice from another room."

And this indelible scene: "As I sank into the leather banquette, the band struck up 'Bewitched.' Next to me was a couple in late middle age, no longer bewitched but enjoying the golden years of a long companionship in the traditional manner: dead silence. A Sotheby's catalog lay on the table between them. The wife, with a back like a ramrod and mouse-colored hair, could have been a small-town librarian, except she wore her reading glasses on top of her head. 'The estate says we'll have the first 10 million by Christmas,' she said. From her tone of voice, she could have been telling a reader the book he wanted was on the third shelf on the right. Her husband, who sported an American flag on his lapel, grunted and continued reading the menu. As if on cue, the music switched to 'La Vie en Rose.'"

Well, I was certain that a confirmed New Yorker like Hodgson would never be lured away to live and review restaurants in Philadelphia, not that the *Inquirer,* to my knowledge, ever considered her. Instead, it hired Craig LaBan from the New Orleans *Times-Picayune.* Blank, with his ear always to the ground, was one of the first to find out. LaBan had studied at La Varenne, Anne Willan's cooking school in Burgundy, so perhaps he knew food. But there was something unsavory, even morbid, in the way he wrote about it. "A fruity splash of . . . olive oil glistens on the meat," he said in one of his first reviews for the *Inquirer.* "Thin strips of

Dover sole, gracefully filleted tableside and arched across the dish, reveal the luxury of their firm ivory flesh against the velvety softness of a light and lemony butter sauce." His imagery, to me, suggested an autopsy.

"Craig LaBan called," Blank told me one day. "He asked me a lot of questions and said his review of Deux Cheminées would appear in a week or two. He said he has eaten just about everything on the menu."

"Did you know he was coming around?"

"I had no idea. Everyone always recognized Eileen because she had been on the beat for so long, and, of course, her photograph appeared with her column. This guy takes pains to be anonymous, I'm told. Anyway, I don't care. I never did anything differently when Eileen showed up in the dining room, and I wouldn't change anything for this fellow either, except put a Whoopee Cushion on his chair."

I was expecting Deux Cheminées to receive four bells, the top rating. Instead LaBan awarded three, which I felt was an injustice. Still, the review was careful and generally enthusiastic, though wordy and rife with malapropisms and tortured metaphors. LaBan wrote, in part, "Fritz Blank is one of those rare individuals who does many things well. Under his tutelage Deux Cheminées has gracefully matured into one of the city's bona fide big-occasion classics. Its sumptuously appointed dining rooms are warmed by six blazing fireplaces, an elegant montage of Victorian art, and fifteen antique clocks, whose chimes and dings and bongs fill the air with the comforting resonance of a private home. Bolstered by an obsessive thirst for books, with a cookbook collection that now exceeds ten thousand, Blank has become one of Philadelphia's preeminent food historians and teaching chefs. Nearly two hundred apprentices have passed through his kitchen over the years, constantly bringing him soups and sauces dabbed on a plate for his tasting scrutiny: 'It's too sweet. It needs more milk.' And they will return until it's perfect."

So far, so good. The art displayed in Deux Cheminées was nei-ther Victorian nor in montage, and a copy editor should have flagged "bolstered by an obsessive thirst for books," but never mind. LaBan went on, "Few chefs, to my mind, could provide lessons in cookery as valuable as Blank's. Though his food is rarely about in-novation, it is technically pristine, a classically rooted repertoire that reflects the depth of his studies: largely creamy, stock-infused French dishes, inflected with the occasional German spaetzle or liver dumpling. His mastery of the focusing of flavors is evident in every rich bite, beginning with unforgettable soups. From the mo-ment his ruefully rich crab soup Marguerite touches the tongue, its béchamel edged by an alcoholic splash of Scotch, nerve endings will tingle down to the end of your toes. His amber dark consommé Celestin is so crystal pure, the ribbons of toasty crepe and snappy fresh peas lend its broth real dynamic. Cauliflower soup is unstop-pably delicious, graced with a whisper of fresh tarragon. And the creamy elixirs of spinach and wild mushroom left me longing for our silent waiter to return so I could finish what was left in the la-dles of those big white soup tureens."

I yearned for relief, however brief, from the lurid descriptions of food. Had the mood in the room been jolly or hushed? Did a birth-day cake appear at another table, or perhaps an engagement ring? (Proposals were a regular occurrence at Deux Cheminées, captain Carlo Cicchini once told me.) A little fresh air, please. But no: "Baked striped bass and steamed salmon were impeccably moist, the bass made exotic by mangoes and a citrusy compote of herbed tomatoes, the salmon practically melting into its dill beurre blanc."

Halfway through, I braced for the caveats and complaints. They came eventually, in this airless paragraph: "Institutions such as Deux Cheminées are priceless in part for the forgotten dishes they perpetuate, the kind that are numerous on this menu. Super-thin slices of calves' liver are crisp, yet medium-rare, anointed in rasp-berry vinegar that is a touch sweet. Tender escargots doused with garlicky Pernod butter come with a warm brioche bun on the side, steamy and soft, to soak up the juices. The silky texture of real Béarnaise sauce transformed an already wonderful New York strip steak into a paragon of meat. Lean and tender frogs' legs were infused with the tang of white-wine verjus and herbaceous juniper berries. Crisp sweetbreads, moist and buttery inside, were steeped in a wine broth with cloves, then napped with a perfect Madeira sauce. What a shame that such a wonderful sauce should be served over a black plate, as all the appetizers are. Not only are the black plates lightweight china—a mild disappointment for these prices, like the Oneida flatware—but they show every finger smudge and can make even a fine sauce look like glue."

I wanted to clue LaBan that Philadelphians don't mind funk with their finery. To us, chintzy china and mid-market cutlery are homey. But wait, what about those "napping" sweetbreads? Did he mean to say they were dozing in an alcoholic stupor caused by the Madeira sauce? Never mind, more serious business was looming:

"It does not help that some of the food—frog's legs; pork in citrus sauce; truffle sauce and beans for the lamb—already are less than hot when the silver presentation bells are removed from the plates. The kitchen is quite a hike, nestled into the basement at the end of a long corridor lined with copper pots. And Deux Cheminées' distinguished black-tie servers don't exactly seem the jogging types. So that might explain it. Yet there was a certain Old World grace in the waiters' unobtrusive manner that I do appreciate. I'll never forget the image of the gallant maître d' standing in the middle of Locust Street until a taxi heeded his statue-like glare and stopped. In the translation of serving, however, this unobtrusiveness felt somewhat stuffy; and at that, there were lapses in refreshing water and a very slow hand on bread. Our second waiter, who had difficulty answering basic menu questions, shocked us when he broke his stoic facade to relate how he had delivered his mother's baby while waiting for the rescue squad to arrive."

At that, my own stoic facade broke. I phoned Blank. "So, your waiter grossed out the reviewer?"

"Yeah, it looks that way."

"What was your man thinking?"

"Beats me. To be fair, it's an interesting story. I've heard him tell it. But obviously it's not for the dining room. I'm more upset over what LaBan said about the black plates and the cold food. The black plates were Neil's idea. He bought them for thirty-nine cents apiece. I hate them. The food looks bad on them, as LaBan said, and they're always covered with fingerprints."

"And the cold food?"

"It's hot when it leaves the kitchen, but then it sits in the waiters' room."

"Whose fault is that?"

"Well, the maître d' is responsible. My partner's afraid of replacing him, but no one is indispensable. If you ever think you can't be replaced, just put your head in a bucket of water and see how big a hole you leave when you pull it out. But I don't want to sound sore. All in all, I think LaBan gave us a really stellar review. I couldn't have been more complimentary if I'd written it myself."

A year passed, during which Hodgson reviewed Lespinasse, an epitome of East Side luxe. She might have been describing Deux Cheminées. "Lespinasse" she said, "could be a three-star entry in the Guide Michelin, circa 1957. It has all the trappings of haute cuisine: an all-male staff of waiters in black tie, six-foot flower arrangements, chandeliers (topped with boudoir lampshades), foie gras and truffles, *amuses-bouches* and petits fours, expensive French china and wineglasses big enough to house a school of goldfish." She concluded," When you get the bill at Lespinasse, it requires the expression that the better sort of aristocrat wore on the way to the guillotine."

In that same period, LaBan wrote: "The beauty of Creole cooking has been its ability to absorb and reflect the ethnic diversity that has settled in southern Louisiana, from the French, Spanish, German, Haitian, and African flavors that crafted its original melting pot to the Vietnamese population that is swelling now." He contorted the noun "truffle" into a verb and astonished me, in one review, by complaining of a guest at his own table who "bellowed with stunning pomposity throughout the evening to a room full of strangers, spouting his dubious views on movies and more than a few unsolicited details of his sex life." (I filed this column under "Believe It or Not," next to a review from the *New York Times* in which William Grimes, having demoted a top chef from four stars to two, gave himself two stars for a dinner he and his wife cooked at home for friends.)

In time, LaBan seemed to get under Blank's skin, too. "What did you think of his review of Danube?" Blank asked me by email. He knew that Risa and I had been to David Bouley's Vienneseish restaurant on Hudson Street in New York. We had loved it. Moira Hodgson had given Danube four stars. LaBan liked it, too, but sneered in passing at the "leaden" cuisine of Austria.

"Why do we need to review restaurants in other cities anyway," Blank wanted to know, "especially when Philadelphia is struggling to hold its own? When are we going to wake up and crawl out from under the cloak of New York? Also, I wonder where LaBan got the notion that Austrian food is heavy and laden with grease. Has he ever been to Vienna? He seems more impressed with posh than substance, and I suspect he had little real dining experience before he became a restaurant critic. I find his writing style and culinary judgment perplexing and arbitrary, though not as wacky as Elaine T.'s. I guess the rain has made me cranky."

One day Blank called to tell me that Craig LaBan had been nominated for a James Beard Foundation Award in the newspaper restaurant review category.

"Get out," I said. "Who is he up against?"

"A New York writer, Moira Hodgson."

"Oh, well, no contest."

"Do you know her?"

"I don't know her but I read her every week. She's a great writer. She studied cooking with Jean-Louis Palladin and really knows her stuff. She's a shoo-in."

"Don't be too sure," Blank said. "The Beard House is full of politics."

He was right. LaBan got the award. At the ceremony, a friend of Blank's happened to be seated at Hodgson's table. The friend emailed Blank that she had been "sweetness personified, until Craig LaBan was announced as the winner in her category. She immediately got up and stomped out."

If Hodgson did in fact stomp out, I don't blame her. She had more experience and understanding of food and restaurants than LaBan did, to say nothing of being, by far, the better writer. Had I been at the award ceremony, I like to think, I would have booed the announcement like a good Philadelphian.

Blank kept up an occasional and always cordial correspondence with LaBan. "Dear Craig," he wrote one day. "I am not one to pinch food writers in the pants, but I feel duty bound to point out that there is nothing 'unusual,' as you put it, about crepinettes." (Reporting on a new French bistro, LaBan had marveled at a plate of veal sausage patties.) "They might be bourgeois, but they can be found on French menus worldwide, even today. *I make them all the time!*

"But my real concern is that we Americans are accelerating gastronomical evolution into warp drive. 'If it ain't new, it's dreck' is the mentality. How sad for us. How soon we forget the delights of even the near past. Quiche Lorraine is as delicious as ever. It is still prepared and served all over Europe, and yet it is eschewed here as 'Jurassic.' I am not against the innovations of 'nouvelle' and 'fusion' cuisine. However, our penchant for 'What's Happenin' Now, Baby?' cooking is almost out of control. New for the sake of newness has dulled our sensibilities. It's gotten to the point that if you don't eat out within a week of when a 'new' dish appears on a menu, it is displaced by something else even newer, and often far from better. Well, I'd best stop for now, lest I spontaneously combust. Thanks for listening to my rant, and please don't take my 'bah, humbug' personally."

15.

Chickens and Eggs

A S TIME PASSED, I attended fewer classes at Deux Cheminées. I had not lost interest, and certainly did not think there was nothing more to learn from Fritz Blank. But Risa's knitwear business was prospering and I was involved in it, traveling with her to sales events, helping to set up the display, and attending to customers. On the road, I learned to improvise in meager hotel kitchenettes. When I did manage to attend a class in Blank's kitchen, it felt like a homecoming. On one of those rare Monday mornings, he was at his customary spot behind the reception desk.

"I'm just back from this year's food writers' conference at the Greenbrier in West Virginia," he told the new assortment of students. "I go every year. So does Julia Child. She was in good form, though she's getting on. People were telling 'Julia' stories, and she told some, too, imitating herself and making fun of her public image. But down to business. Did you all get your recipe handouts? You'll see that we're doing three things today—the rack of lamb that we've always served at the restaurant but with a different sauce, a Bordelaise; then *pommes de terre Anna*—sliced potatoes baked in butter—and rainbow trout with a tarragon butter sauce called *sauce Colbert*. It's named for a minister in the court of Louis Quatorze, not Claudette Colbert the actress. Claudette Colbert had a house next to ours on Fire Island, but I never cooked with her."

Breakfast was ready downstairs as usual, and so were our chairs, lined up in the aisle opposite the stoves. Blank took his position in the other aisle, speaking to us across the long central island that served as his podium.

"Notice that this trout has a pinkish color," he said, holding up a fish by its gills. "That's because it was farm-raised on crayfish. They're sometimes called salmon trout. I chose the recipe we're using today because it shows the simplicity of the French way of cooking fish. At the Greenbrier, Julia Child and Anne Willan demonstrated a basic French housewife's fish recipe from the 1920s. Everyone in the audience kept suggesting stuff to add to it, mostly for presentation, and Julia got livid. She said, 'We're losing our taste sense. Everything is becoming audiovisual.' She meant that food these days is too often prepared for eye appeal, for decoration rather than for savor.

"You should cook trout with the head on, even if you don't intend to serve it that way, because oil glands in the head help the flavor. The rule of thumb for cooking fish, according to the Canadian Board of Fisheries, is ten minutes per inch of thickness." He placed the trout in the convection oven and turned his attention to the lamb.

"The rack is from the rib area, between the shoulder and loin. Have your butcher French the rack and trim the fat and silver skin, or do the trimming yourself. Get all the fat off because it congeals more than chicken or pork fat. Cooking it is straightforward. We marinate the rack for fifteen or twenty minutes in a mixture of soy sauce, mustard, olive oil, and herbs—it's on the recipe sheets I gave you; a batch will keep in the fridge almost forever—and then we finish it with *sauce Périgord,* made with Madeira and truffles. But today, as I said, I'm making a *bordelaise,* which is red wine, shallots, veal or beef stock, and cracked black peppercorns. Oh, and a teaspoon or two of sugar. Georges Perrier showed me that trick a hundred years ago—'eet take away zee aceed.' Georges was in a film once, '*Les Trucs des Chefs,*' in which a bunch of chefs each had thirty seconds to show off some favorite cooking trick. All the others tried to do complicated stuff. Georges just put sugar in red wine sauce. That was it."

Blank produced a mandoline from under the island and made

ready to slice potatoes. I admired this ingenious hand-operated device, with blades adjustable to modulate thickness. To this day, however, I'm timid about using one for fear of slicing my knuckles along with the spuds. The chef made easy work of it, layering the potato slices in a buttered skillet while adding more butter between the layers. Then he placed a weighted cover directly on the potatoes and put the skillet in the oven.

He checked the progress of the fish. "Not quite. We have a few minutes to kill. I'll tell you a Julia story I heard at the Greenbrier. A food writer from Atlanta said she was traveling with Julia somewhere in the South when they stopped at a McDonalds. Yes, Julia Child sometimes eats at the arches, and she's also been known to pack peanut butter and jelly sandwiches when she flies. Anyway, they drove into the parking lot and got out of the car to go inside. A street repair crew was working nearby with roaring jackhammers, and Julia said something like, 'What a terrible racket, I wish they would stop,' whereupon the jackhammers did stop and six big burly men put down their machines and looked at Julia. 'Oh, dear,' Julia said, 'do you suppose they heard me? Did I make them mad?' Even more alarming, before she could duck inside the McDonalds, they all hurried over, and the biggest of them came right up to her with a kind of grimace on his face. 'Oh, Julia,' he said, 'the last time I tried your recipe for duck à l'orange. . .' and he launched into a description of some problem he'd had at the stove. They all listened attentively while Julia gave him some tips that apparently cleared up his problem, and the whole crew went cheerfully back to work."

I came early to the second class in the series to help with kitchen preparations. Blank said he was feeling grumpy. A crew from *Philadelphia* magazine was due later that day for a Thanksgiving-themed photo shoot, but Blank's staff had forgotten to order the turkey. And he had quarreled with his partner about hiring a chef to be second-in-command; a talented chef named Shola Olunloyo was interested and available, but they didn't want to add another salary to the restaurant's budget.

"Shola was an apprentice here, and then he went to work for Perrier," Fritz said. "I heard that Georges considers him the best *charcuterière* in his restaurant. But he doesn't treat him well. They don't get along. He's offered Shola *garde-manger,* which is fairly menial for someone with Shola's ability. We can hire him away if we match the salary. My partners just don't understand the value of expertise."

The day's topics included foie gras and mashed potatoes. "There's a misconception about foie gras," Blank said. "The birds aren't really force-fed, but they're fed so much, and so frequently, that they become habituated to gorging. They crave and demand more. Just like humans. When you saute foie gras, you have to do it quickly, or the fat will burn off. And when you eat it, I suggest you first taste just the pâté, then take some pâté with spinach, and then eat some with spinach and toast. As for the potatoes, when you're cooking in quantity, it's best to steam them so you don't get raw centers, as can happen when they're boiled in water. Idaho potatoes are the best for mashing. After steaming I use a ricer or a Mouli food mill to mash them. Don't put potatoes in a blender; you'll get glue."

From the commonplace potato, Blank proceeded, in his third class of the series, to eggs—"known and feared in my profession as one of the most difficult foods to cook. Even hard-cooked eggs, or hard-boiled if you prefer, are tricky. Lots of chefs and home cooks, including my late mother—sorry, Mom—do a bad job of it by overcooking, making rubbery whites and dry, greenish-blue yolks that smell of sulfur. If you follow the instructions on your handout, you'll make hard-cooked eggs that are delicious, tender, attractive, and don't smell like dog farts." (The instructions said, "Place fresh whole 'extra large' chicken eggs in an accommodating sauce pan and cover with cold water exactly one inch above the tops of the eggs. Place the pan over HIGH heat and bring quickly to a full rolling boil. Remove the pan from the heat and cover it with a lid. Set a timer for ten minutes. Prepare an ice slurry bath using plenty of ice and just enough cold water to allow the ice to move freely. After the eggs have steeped for ten minutes, remove them quickly from the hot water with a large slotted spoon or a 'spider' and immediately plunge them into the ice bath. Keep in ice water until ready to peel.")

From hard-cooked eggs, we moved on to omelets. "They're tricky, too," Blank said. "Most omelets served in U.S. restaurants are bastardized and banal. My friend Louis Szathmary used to say about dumplings, they're not a recipe, they're technology. The same is true of omelets. I use an iron saute pan, which is much better than aluminum. If you buy a new pan, season it with lard and salt and put it in a 400- to 450-degree oven for about an hour. In any event, heat a seasoned pan over medium-high heat and drop in a tablespoon of butter. In a bowl, beat three eggs and a splash of water thirty-three times. That may sound silly to be so exact, but the butter and eggs should be ready at the same time, and thirty-three whisks with a fork seem to be just about right."

He poured the eggs into the center of the pan. Taking the pan by its handle, he quickly shook and stirred while the eggs set, then added a tablespoon or so of shredded Gruyère. With his fork he folded the omelet, then flipped it onto a warmed plate and rubbed the top with butter. "The first omelet you make," he said, "is like your first crepe; it usually doesn't turn out as well as the ones that follow." This one looked fine to me.

"Now we go from egg to chicken," Blank said. "I want to show you how I brine poultry before I cook it. As food scientists like Harold McGee and Shirley Corriher will tell you, brining makes meat juicier by increasing the liquid held in the cells. If you want to learn more about it, see Shirley's book *Cookwise*. Anyway, I cover the bird with a solution of two-thirds cup noniodized salt per quart of cold water and refrigerate it for about three hours. While it's in the fridge, I make a basting solution of one-third oil—Crisco, for example—and one-third dry liqueur, such as Cognac, sherry, or Armagnac, and one-third chicken stock."

Blank lined up several chickens he had brined in advance and waved a cheesecloth over them in the manner of a stage magician performing a trick. "Be sure to rinse the salt off the meat," he said, "then dip the cheesecloth in the basting mixture and wrap your bird, starting low and working up. Once it's in the oven, baste every seven minutes or so to keep it from drying out.

"Now, for the gravy, take the wing tips, gizzard, heart, belly fat, and neck, and cut them in small pieces and saute them—in duck fat, if you have it—until they're brown. Add chicken stock, or a bouillon cube dissolved in water, plus some chopped carrot, celery, and onion—more of the carrot than the others—and simmer for an hour, adding water when necessary. Then strain it and make a roux. You can avoid lumpy gravy by whisking butter with flour or by making a slurry with equal parts cornstarch and flour.

"So now we've done the chicken and the egg, except for one item. Has anyone noticed? The chicken liver. You don't cook the liver with the other ingredients for the gravy. The liver would make the gravy cloudy. Instead you saute it and eat it when no one is looking."

As I wrote down Blank's instructions, comments, and caveats, often in the margins of the recipe sheets he distributed, I noticed that most others in the class did so, too. As Blank himself said, "I learned long ago to write everything down. Early on, I would make seasonal things and the customers and staff would say, 'This is the best ever.' I thought, 'There's no way in hell I will forget how I made this.' But I did forget. So I started writing down." The home cooks listening and watching him from the other side of the work island got his message. We understood that the world of cooking teemed with well-meant advice, but how many of those tips had been tested for decades by a persnickety chef-scientist? Here are more of them:

• "Soup making," Blank said, "is usually a matter of layering, beginning, say, with sweating onions in the soup pot. Then you put in the heavier vegetables—carrots, rutabagas, parsnips, and etcetera. Celery, shredded cabbage, and other lighter, leafy vegetables come later. The liquid, which goes in last, should be three inches above the top of the solids. By the way, I've never made a bad soup."

• "When you make soup stock, don't boil it down too much, especially if it's poultry, or you'll end up with something that tastes like bacteriological media."

• "Salt masks bitterness and enhances sweetness—on a melon, for example."

• "The best canned tomatoes are from San Marzano. They grow in volcanic soil, near Naples."

• "I make my own chef's salt. To six pounds of salt, I add six tablespoons of sweet paprika, a tablespoon of ground allspice, a tablespoon each of white pepper and black pepper, and a half-teaspoon of garlic salt. That's a restaurant-sized supply of it, of course, so scale down the proportions as you wish."

• "Don't be too snooty about commercial products. Kitchen Bouquet, for instance, can perk up any gravy. Escoffier would have loved it. A tablespoon of Kitchen Bouquet mixed with a tablespoon of olive oil is great for grilling. You can make a mediocre steak taste like a million bucks. By the way, I don't put salt and pepper on my steak until it's on the table."

• "We Philadelphians make the best mashed potatoes, with black pepper. It looks dirty but tastes better than white pepper, which has a more musty flavor."

• "If you put yourself in the right frame of mind when you kill what you eat, you should have no problem. Sometimes I have to scold apprentices when they tease crabs before killing them. By the way, if you buy crabmeat, make sure it hasn't been washed, which makes it tasteless."

• "When poaching, bring the water to 180 or 190 but not to a boil, which tightens the protein. If you want the poaching liquid to have flavor, start the cooking in cold water."

• "Everyone should be able to make a *pâté à choux* at a moment's

notice out of butter, water, flour, and eggs. You can use it for cream
puffs, eclairs, and dumplings, such as *quenelles de brochette."*

• "Anchovy paste, as a seasoning, can really pick up a dish."

• "Mix apple butter with cottage cheese," he told a Jewish student who said she didn't like cottage cheese by itself. "It's kosher
and it's good. This Passover I'm going to a friend's seder, though
I'm not Jewish. The only faith I have is in physics."

• " If you don't have a fat separator, swirl the liquid while tilting
the vessel, then ladle the fat from the 'wake.'"

Blank taught one fall class seated at the big table in the staff
dining room. He was having more trouble with his legs and, for a
few weeks, could not stand up to cook. I was suddenly aware of the
passage of time. Perhaps others were as well. Only two in the class
were new to the group. Some among us had attended every year
since the classes began, nearly a decade before. Today, at least, we
would not have the familiar sight of Blank rumbling around in
front of the stoves, arms high, elbows bent, moving his head left
and right, ready for action—or, as it sometimes seemed, imitating
Sylvester the cat tiptoeing up on Tweety Bird.

Because Blank would not be cooking, our topic was apples. We
began by tasting ten varieties, from Braeburn to Cortland to Rome.
We learned that apples, along with pears and pomegranates, belong
to the rose family. We heard how pears, unlike apples, ripen from
the inside out and must therefore be picked unripe. To speed ripen-
ing, Blank said, place pears near bananas or pineapples and test for
readiness by squeezing their necks. A pear that's too soft will have
flesh that seems gritty.

Blank cut the apples and passed out slices. The Granny Smith
and the Cortland were, to me, a little tart. The Red Delicious was
tasty but with astringency in its skin. The Cortland makes good
applesauce, Blank said, and the Red and Golden Delicious are good

to cook with. I found the Gala and Fuji especially tasty but was not happy to hear from Blank that both varieties are genetically engineered. My favorite of all was the Macoum, a variety unfamiliar to me but not to Blank.

"Macoum is my favorite eating apple," he said with a dreamy look. "It always tastes like autumn to me."

The Inconstant Helper

"COOKS GET HUMILIATED about being below stairs. They have an uneasy feeling that smells—of fish stock, burnt oil, or cabbage soup—hang about them no matter how much they wash, and they get complexes about being pushed out of sight and in general treated as cockroaches."

Nicolas Freeling wrote that in *The Kitchen*, his sardonic remembrance of toiling in European restaurants before he attained more-congenial work writing mysteries. I detected none of that rueful below-stairs mood at Deux Cheminées, perhaps because it was generally understood that Blank was a chef by choice and not by grinding necessity. A microbiologist with a stellar résumé, he was in a position to say, as he sometimes did, "I can always go back to saving lives and stomping out disease." He took his work seriously, of course, and charged himself with maintaining his kitchen's high standards, but he was not the sort of chef one reads about or watches on television who thrives on pain and hysteria. Most paid workers at Deux Cheminées were happy enough to stay on year after year, and students at the Restaurant School considered Deux Cheminées a plum place to apprentice. It was not unusual to find volunteers working in Chef Blank's kitchen, such as Freddy Salpesi, who baked there for the fun of it, and Lisa and Pete, who helped Blank and Yvette Knight with prep chores. And there were the occasional helpers like me who might visit the chef and be invited to put on an apron, or be conscripted for a special occasion, such as a Book and the Cook event or one of Blank's fundraisers for the Philadelphia Singers.

I stopped by the restaurant one day shortly before Easter and found him sitting at the pantry table, cutting dark Italian salami into small rectangles.

"I'm cutting 'batons' for *pizza rustica,* Easter pie," he said. "It's bad form to be sitting down, but my knees are bothering me." He sharpened a knife and handed it to me, along with a portion of uncut salami. "Now, don't cut yourself."

I promptly nicked the tip of my left thumb, which oozed a little blood. Blank didn't see this, and I was too embarrassed to tell him. I just dabbed at the cut now and then with a bit of paper towel and ate the few pieces of salami that had blood on them. The Easter pie, I knew, would be eaten *en famille,* not served in the restaurant, so I figured I wasn't endangering the general population.

Sometimes Blank let me know he would be short-handed for cooking class, which was his oblique way of asking for help. I would arrive early, arrange chairs, photocopy recipes, and help set out breakfast in the pantry. I particularly liked to make Blank's scrambled eggs, which were done in a big bain-marie by a slow process that required a lot of stirring—beaten eggs and a disgraceful amount of butter, into which he might throw asparagus just cooked on the stove. One morning Blank asked me to mix up a breakfast concoction of apricot, honey, yogurt, and orange-peel. Then, with a mortar and pestle, I was to grind a quantity of mysterious black seeds and stir them into the mixture "by titration."

"Titration? What's that?" To be ignorant in Blank's presence no longer embarrassed me.

"For our purposes, it means add to taste."

"And what are the seeds?"

"Cardamom, from the ginger family."

At times, a day in the Deux Cheminées kitchen resembled the routines in my own house. "Where's my folder?" Blank might ask, referring to recipes he had assembled for a particular event. Risa and I were always looking for missing papers, too, it seemed, and, as at Deux Cheminées, the fugitive document was usually found, eventually, two floors away. The difference was that Blank could dispatch someone to find the missing item.

And there were the periodic squalls, as on the day Blank asked an apprentice to place a container of chicken pieces in ice. Misunderstanding him, the apprentice put the ice right in the container with the chicken. "No, no, no, no, no, NO! Blank yelled. "The ice will melt in there and ruin the flavor of the chicken." Within a minute, he was apologizing for raising his voice.

In addition to the annual composer dinners at Deux Cheminées, Blank staged other fundraising events for the Philadelphia Singers, away from the restaurant. This involved considerable arranging and transporting, so the roomy van that Risa and I drove to craft shows was put to use. One year, a crew of volunteers and I delivered provender to the enormous atrium of the University of the Arts. The fundraiser, well attended, was addressed by actor Tony Randall, visiting from New York.

"I never come to Philadelphia without remembering a flop from my early days," he told the crowd. "We opened in Boston to frightful reviews, but when we brought the show to Philadelphia, I was heartened when I got to the theater and saw a long line for the box office. It turned out they were getting their money back. We did a matinee on Christmas day for an audience of about twelve. At the end, I took my bow, to scarcely any applause, and said, 'Merry Christmas.' A voice came back, 'Go to hell.' But Philadelphia made up for it by giving me Jack Klugman, my housemate and tormentor in 'The Odd Couple.' He was born here, you know."

Another year, we filled the van at the service door on Camac Street and drove across town to the Restaurant School, where Blank staged an indoor picnic in the school's big central court. At times like this, when he ventured from the restaurant with his food, he could be inattentive and forgetful, as when he forgot to bring a saute pan to a cooking demonstration on public television. On this day, I was with Shola Olunloyo, Blank's friend and protégé. As Blank wandered off to schmooze with guests, Olunloyo, without orders, took immediate command of the Restaurant School kitchen. (I had come to admire how kitchen professionals so often jumped into a fray unasked in order to keep a meal from going awry.) As it turned out, Blank's pepper slaw had been left behind. I drove back to retrieve it and then made a second run to fetch a platter of pulled pork from another participating restaurant. (Its kitchen, compared with Blank's, was filthy). Before I knew it, the food had been served, the guests had eaten their fill, and it was time to clean up. Had I eaten? I couldn't remember. I put on an apron and bussed plates, moving among the paying guests for whom my servitude rendered me invisible. I had to remind myself that on most occasions, I was one of those heedless ones being served.

I felt closest to Nicolas Freeling's self-pitying kitchen wretches the time Blank received the Distinguished Alumnus award from his alma mater, Delaware Valley College of Science and Agriculture, in Doylestown, Pennsylvania. As he put it to me, "I have been selected for the Alumni Association's Achievement Award for Science. I'll be able to cash it in for . . . nothing whatever, except to hang it on the wall." As often happens when a group bestows an honor on a chef, the honoree is asked to provide the food. So on a spring afternoon, a half-dozen fellow recruits and I loaded the van once more and drove forty miles north to Doylestown, in Bucks County. This time, while Blank socialized with his classmates and other well-wishers, I told the younger helpers what to do, playing the Shola role with all the authority I could summon. I was in full kitchen regalia—checked pants, chef's tunic—and feeling rather self-important when a diner waved me over and pointed at her water glass.

"It's empty. Can't you *see?*"

When we got back to Deux Cheminées, dinner service was over, and the line cooks were preparing to leave for the night. They seemed amused as we trucked in leftovers and empty food containers.

"You have your catering faces on," one of them said.

"And what's a catering face?"

"You look like zombies. Hungry, miserable zombies."

I did not have the time to help with any more events away from the restaurant. I was not indispensable, of course, and Blank forged on to raise money for the Singers. One year he roasted a pig at a friend's farm but was disappointed with the turnout. "The pig roast was a lot of work for the same cast of folks who always end up being the worker bees," he wrote to the charity's director. "The event was almost too casual, and the few attendees—less than 100—yielded watery soup. Still it was a party, and everyone got plenty to eat. Maybe we captured some new supporters. Since a few of us footed most of the cost, the $2,000 or so we took in is revenue for the Singers. I know, I know, it's a drop in the bucket, but let's not kick a gift horse in the ass."

The annual Book and the Cook dinners gave me a chance to gain experience in Blank's kitchen and watch other chefs at work. One morning I went upstairs to his library to find a book and was startled to see, in the dimness at the far end of the room, a very small person, shoeless and wearing an oversized white sweater. It was not a wayward child or a spirit from another realm, but Eileen Yin-Fei Lo, who was in town with her husband, the food writer Fred Ferretti, to oversee preparations for a dinner based on her new work, *The Chinese Kitchen*. Eileen and Fred, good friends of Blank's, were staying in the Deux Cheminées guest quarters. Within minutes, I was doing chores for Eileen down in Blank's kitchen, chopping onions and trimming the legs from several hundred shrimp. Her energy and focus were remarkable. She always seemed to know what to do next and never hesitated to ask for help. Often she needed nothing more than to have something fetched from a shelf beyond her reach. "Eileen put on my kitchen like a glove," Blank said.

As she relates in *The Chinese Kitchen*, she was raised in upper-class surroundings near Canton. "I remember my father, Lo Pak Wan, my first cooking teacher, telling me that we must eat our food first with our eyes, then with our minds, then with our noses, and finally with our mouths. 'Keep an open mind,' he would say. 'If you keep walking only in a straight line, you will go into a wall. You must learn to make a turn if necessary. Do not be narrow.' Or he would tell me an aphorism that translates as, 'If you don't have a tail, you cannot imitate the monkey; if you do have a tail, then do not imitate the monkey.' By this he was telling me to follow the classical manner but not to be a simple, mindless imitator."

A grandmother also tutored her. "My Ah Paw knew instinctively, without ever having had to personally put a spatula into a wok, how things ought to be cooked, what foods wedded in combination, and what clashed. She would eat no vegetables that were older than two hours out of the ground, which necessitated repeated trips to the markets by her servants, a lesson in the importance of freshness that was not lost on me. Do not shout in the kitchen, Ah Paw would insist. Do not use improper words. Do not show shortness of temper by, for example, banging chopsticks on a wok. All of these would reflect badly on us as a family, she would say, when done in front of Jo Kwan, the kitchen god, whose image hung on the wall over the oven."

Preparing her "Feast for the Year of the Dragon" at Deux Cheminées, which consumed nearly a week, Eileen cut poultry with a knife as long as her forearm—aim, whack, aim whack—laughing as goo splattered. She peeled garlic with a cleaver and used its handle like a mortar. "This has been a revelation to me," Blank said. "The technique is so different, but still I can sense the culinary canon behind every dish. There are so many nuances. When Eileen and I went shopping in Chinatown, she would say, 'Don't buy that. I don't like the brand.'"

Eileen's Year of the Dragon feast involved ten courses, starting with "Three Little Sisters" and progressing to "Seven Older Sisters." I was amazed by it all, especially the steamed striped bass and soy noodles. I sat with Fred Ferretti and two young men who often volunteered at the restaurant. I wanted to know how he and

Eileen had met, and how he had pried her away from her tradition-bound family.

"I was in the Army," he said, "on leave in Hong Kong. She was managing in the shop of an Indian tailor. I kept going back to the shop for more shirts, a jacket, and trousers over the period of my leave, but she was from a good family and wouldn't go out with me. One day I followed her onto the bus as she was going home, and she agreed to have tea. Eventually she agreed to go to dinner, but with a chaperone. A year later we were married in Hong Kong. I loved her and admired her strength. She's so strong she didn't have much trouble adjusting to life in the U.S. We live in a fifteen-room house in northern New Jersey with collections of prints and porcelain, and have two sons and a daughter. The oldest son became a chef and teaches at the Restaurant School in Philadelphia. I like to cook but don't often. When I make something with Eileen's leftovers, she will say, 'What you doing with my food?'"

Before the evening was over, Ferretti told me, "This is the best-ever presentation of Eileen's cooking." A group of Chinese émigrés, visiting Philadelphia from Alabama, told Blank they had never eaten so well outside of Hong Kong.

For another Book and the Cook event, Blank was paired with Jessica Harris, whose *The Africa Cookbook* was just out. Together they planned a "Night in Casablanca" based on Harris's recipes from Morocco.

"I've bought fezzes for the waiters," Blank told me. "And, since you've been to Morocco, what do you think of red sashes? Or should they be pink?"

"Use red," I said. "Pink is for some other night."

"Pink is every night here."

Blank had solicited the help of Esther Press McManus, who was Moroccan by birth. And she in turn provided one of her employees,

Hussein Aggour, to oversee the prep work. On the first day of preparation, Aggour showed Blank how to make mint tea, with lots of virtuosic pouring and swirling. My first job for him was to toast almonds in a heavy saute pan, which I tried to do carefully. Still, Aggour had to correct me several times: "Turn up the heat a little; don't put so many almonds in the pan at once." Meanwhile, he started a *bastila,* made with phyllo, pigeon, and poussin. He let me taste the delicious *harira* he was making, a soup into which he put ginger powder, cumin, paprika, turmeric, lentils, cilantro, chickpeas, and crushed tomatoes.

"*Harira* is a national dish," he said. "During Ramadan it is served in every house for breakfast, and in every house it is a little different. Of course, my mother made the best *harira,* so now I make it best."

Aggour was from Midelt, a market town on a plateau of the Middle Atlas Mountains. He told me, "Back home the housewife takes her bread dough to be baked in the public oven. My mother got tired of doing this, so without telling my father, she bought a gas oven and had it installed upstairs in the kitchen, where my father never goes. After a few days of eating her bread baked at home, my father said, 'There must be someone new at the public oven because this bread doesn't taste as good.' My mother confessed, and my father told her to get rid of the oven. So now it's on the roof of their house, and a chicken is living in it."

On the second day of preparation, Esther said, "Fritz's kitchen is so harmonious. It's a pleasure to be here." She was working at a fryer, making dessert. "Marcella Hazan used to say that frying is an art. She was horrible to me. Victor, her husband, was even worse. But I owe her my understanding of Italian food, and her books have been very important here. Why can't everyone be as nice as Fritz?"

The next evening Risa and I went to Deux Cheminées for the "Soirée à Casablanca" that had taken three days to prepare. Hussein was in the lobby, wearing a jacket and bloomer-like pants of fine white material trimmed in gold.

"I wore this when I worked in the king's palace in Rabat," he said. "The palace was from another time, a city inside a city. First you had the palace itself and around it the quarters of the Africans, then the neighborhood of the Jews—referred to as the salt sellers—and finally the Moroccan majority, Arab and Berber."

Our table was in the Gold Room. Lamplight from Camac Street put an amber glow on the lace curtains. The waiters, free of tuxedo jackets for the evening, seemed to be enjoying their red tarbouches and sashes. One of them brought a plate of appetizers: tiny carrots, olives, peppers, and cauliflower with lots of crunch and piquancy. Next came the *harira*, with a suggestion from the waiter to take a bite of date before each spoonful of soup. After an intermezzo of orange slices dipped in cinnamon, we were served the *bastila*, described on the menu as "a layered composition of savory and sweet squab, poussin, and almonds, laced with a cinnamon-coriander custard wrapped in *pâté à brique.*" It tasted convincingly of Morocco to Risa and me, reminding us of a dinner we had forged through at a sumptuous restaurant in Marrakesh, valiantly but wrongheadedly trying to eat everything on the enormous platters set before us. This time, the *bastila* did not arrive in a big communal dish but in little pies. Mine was singed on the bottom, which was the result, Aggour told me later, of some miscreant using butter instead of oil in frying. Still, I ate the *bastila* with pleasure, as well as the *lamb tajine* that came after.

Jessica Harris, tall and elegant in a black kaftan trimmed in gold, made the rounds of the dining rooms. Risa and I had first met her at a Book and the Cook event several years before, on publication of *The Welcome Table*, which I had come to use often. She and Blank were close, and she often stayed in his guest quarters when she was in Philadelphia. She came over and accepted an offered chair.

"It's good to sit. I had to teach an English class early this morning, so I've been up what feels like forever. But life is good. I've bought a house in New Orleans, in the French Quarter. I plan to move down in May. And I've got another book to do on the cuisine of what I call Atlantic Rim," the east coast of the Americas.

Esther, wearing a kaftan and headband, made the rounds, too, accepting the applause of the diners. "Fritz's kitchen is the best organized I've ever worked in," she told us. As for Blank, I found him sitting with Aggour in the lobby, wearing a tarbouche and looking happy but exhausted. "Congratulations," I said to them. Then, facetiously, "I thought the toasted almonds were especially good."

In the Weeds

Chefs come in two sizes, very fat or very thin.
—Wallis Callahan of Coventry Forge Inn,
Pottstown, Pa.

*A*LTHOUGH BLANK HAD JOKED years before about the Philadelphia river flowing from the tears of its chefs, over time I saw him shed real tears only twice, both while listening to Christmas carols, a mitigating circumstance, it seemed to me. Apart from his complaining, endemic to Philadelphians, I found him stoic, able to withstand considerable pain, both physical and emotional.

I once phoned him the day before he was to give a talk at St. Joseph's University. "I'm hurting," he said. "I had some warts removed from my perineum—you know, that spot between your legs, just behind the balls. They numbed me up and told me it would drain and hurt like hell. I said, 'Yeah, yeah, big deal.' I was being Major Blank, the soldier-medic. Of course, they were right, and here I am without enough pain-killer. I feel like I sat on a hornets' nest."

"So, are you taking the day off? Have you canceled your talk for tomorrow?"

"Are you kidding? Why would I?" And then he changed the subject. A talented apprentice, Adam Becker, had maxed his cooking demonstration exam at the Restaurant School. Blank was clearly proud of him. "I told Adam, 'Stay cool, don't prepare too much for it in advance; just pretend you're cooking something for your mother.'"

Another time, Blank told me he had just been diagnosed with

fulminating cellulitis. "I recognized the symptoms and went to the doctor yesterday. My legs feel like they'd been dipped in boiling oil. The fronts of them are the color of overripe plums. It's an opportunist infection peculiar to diabetics, and there's no cure at hand, so it's also painful knowing it will continue. I'm falling apart."

The cellulitis continued to pester Blank, but he did not fall apart. He phoned me from Thomas Jefferson Hospital early one morning to say he'd gone in hours before with a flare-up of the cellulitis and a temperature of 104. Four days later he was home, hooked up to an intravenous drip and sitting with his legs elevated. A dismal few weeks followed. The codeine he took for pain relief kept him awake at night. His legs cracked open and oozed. He was obliged to miss the Oxford Symposium, at which, with Marcie Pelchat, he would have presented a paper and given a demonstration on taste, smell, and memory. At the same time, the young daughter of one of the kitchen staff had been diagnosed with leukemia. ("I love her. I call her every day in Children's Hospital. She can cook like a dream.") Even Blank's cat, usually a reliable source of companionship and comfort, was out of sorts; she had somehow put her tail in the wrong place at the wrong time—under the toilet seat as Blank sat down on it. According to him, she yelled bloody murder and shunned him for days.

For a brief time, when the cellulitis was most pernicious, Blank thought about replacing himself as chef de cuisine, even closing Deux Cheminées. "But it's been a gift to have the restaurant," he told me, "and I don't want it to end." A week after leaving the hospital, he was back in the pantry, doing prep work as always and filling in for Yvette, the day chef, who was out sick. He continued with his cooking classes, too.

Despite his physical courage and his ability to endure bodily pain, Blank seemed powerless in one aspect. He once showed me a photograph of himself in close-fitting chefs' whites, standing in front of the first Deux Cheminées building, on Camac Street. "That's me in the old days. Can you believe it? I did sit-ups every day to keep my waist trim." The difference between the slender man in the picture, aged thirty-five or so, and the Blank of twenty years later was astonishing. He said, "I'm pretty careful about what I eat most of the day, but evenings are my downfall. Then I become compulsive."

It was clear that his busy workdays kept Blank's mind occupied with the tasks of the moment. But when the day was over and his staff and customers had departed, he became the lone occupant of a large Victorian building at the heart of a big and often-impersonal city. That was when the painful memories invaded, along with worries about his future, and he turned for solace to the food he kept in the galley-kitchen at the far end of his library, next to the private den where he had his work desk and computer, his lounge chair, and television. Food, in place of booze, was his nightly binge.

To be fair, there was sufficient cause to seek oblivion in potato chips and nuts and leftovers and pizza and Chinese take-out after a full day of tasting his restaurant's meals. The death of his mentor Louis Szathmary, for example, was followed by a succession of upsetting events. Blank lost his friend Nicholas Kurti, the Oxford physicist and founder of the Erice symposia on science and gastronomy. Then Blank and his staff were shocked when one of the waiters went home one evening and found his roommate murdered in their bed. And not long after that, he got the horrifying news that his friend, the cheese merchant Claudio Auriemma, had killed himself in the presence of his estranged girlfriend.

"Claudio used to be heavy-set and loud, with a repertoire of great one-liners," Blank told me. "But when I saw him a few weeks ago, he'd lost fifty pounds and looked drawn. I asked about the girlfriend and he said, 'No, I'm not seeing her anymore.' Apparently he called her up and asked her to come over and blew his brains out in front of her. Suicide is about the most selfish act there is."

Perhaps worse than such jolts were the daily aggravations. Blank once told me, "I'm being nibbled to death by ducks, as Groucho Marx used to say. Brian, my line chef, got into a fight with one of the apprentices. I'd seen it coming for weeks, and then it flared up

with shouting and threats. I made them stop immediately. I don't
put up with that. I told them to go calm down for fifteen minutes
and then meet me in the office. When they came in, I said I would-
n't tolerate fighting. They had let things go too far to ever be
friends, but they had to be civil to each other. I made them shake
hands. Brian said, 'I don't wanna, but I'll do it 'cause you said so.'
So, what was my reward for peacemaking? I found out that Fodor's,
which runs the Mobil travel guides now, has demoted us from four
stars to three. No explanation; they no longer send reviewers, just
depend on the judgment of local freelancers—and some have axes
to grind."

To his credit, Blank also found comfort in more-wholesome
ways than evening food binges. He had a repertoire of jokes and
one-liners that he would recite with little prompting, or distribute
to his email list.

Q: What do you call a three-legged cow?

A: Lean beef.

Q. What do you call a cow with no hind legs?

A: Ground beef.

There were hundreds more, most of them better than those,
some worse. Many were off-color or mocked the political shenani-
gans in Washington, D.C., which he called "that squirrel cage."
And many jokes were recycled from the internet. "I seem to be on
every cyber-joke list in the country," he told Harold McGee. "I try
to screen them all and send only the better ones to my buddies."

And there was the solace of gossip, most especially scuttlebutt
about the misadventures of colleagues. "I was in the Reading Terminal this morning," Blank said once, "and I ran into Jack Mc-
David—you know, the self-styled bumpkin who has a diner there
plus a restaurant near London Grill. Well, he had two black eyes
and one arm was in a sling. I said, 'What happened to you?' He said,
'I had dealings with someone.' He wouldn't elaborate. I have ears
and eyes around town, so I got the scoop later. It started in the dining room of his restaurant when he shoved one of his waiters—don't

ask me why. The waiter said, 'Please don't do that.' McDavid shoved him again. The waiter goes, 'I said, Don't do that. Don't do it again.' McDavid shoves a third time, and the waiter says, 'I quit.' So then McDavid starts cussing out the waiter in front of the customers. The waiter is bigger and stronger than McDavid, and finally just beats the shit out of him. The customers had to break it up because the staff was howling with laughter, and none would intervene."

The excitable Georges Perrier also provided grist for gossip. Blank emailed, "The buzz here is that Georges fell down the basement stairs of a neighbor's house and fractured both legs. Unlike the finger-nipping episode [Perrier nearly lost the fingers of his right hand to a mechanical slicer], he's trying to keep this one hush-hush. Supposedly he consults a psychic and is convinced this is the work of demons sent by a rival—not me—to drive him out of business. I think the poor man has gone absolutely nuts!"

A more-uplifting pastime was his devotion to vocal music, which he played at high volume in his library. He faithfully attended Philadelphia Singers concerts, even when the Singers went out of town to perform, say, with the New York Philharmonic. I once attended a Singers' Christmas program with him in the neo-Romanesque sanctuary of St. Clement's Church. Named for the fourth pope of Rome, who was martyred in A.D. 100, St. Clement's was high church Episcopal. The clergy and much of the congregation were gay, Blank told me—"they use more incense than anyone else." He and I sat in a pew directly in front of Kathleen Mulhern, owner of the Garden Restaurant. "I guess this is Restaurant Row," Blank told her. The Singers performed the main program from the front of the sanctuary, concluding with Gustav Holst's *Psalm 148*. Then they filed into the side aisles to lead the audience through three familiar carols. Blank cried all the way through "O Come All Ye Faithful." Several times his body quaked with sobs. He was not embarrassed by this and merely said, "It was my mother's favorite Christmas song."

After the concert, we walked a few blocks to a reception for the

Singers and their principal financial backers. Some of the performers had girths that rivaled Blank's, and I soon discovered that a few
of them had formed an eating group with their chef-benefactor. He
once emailed me: "Tonight I shall join a riotous party at Pine Street
Pizza with David Hayes [the Singers' music director] and a handful
of the PSFS group [Philadelphia Singers Food-lovers' Society], a.k.a.
the Happy Heavyweights, a.k.a. the Fat Ladies' *Sängerfest*. This is
to thank David for his part in the Singers becoming the official cho-
rus of the Philadelphia Orchestra. Ciao, Fritz-the-Fat."

(Fritz-the-Fat was just one of the nicknames Blank gave himself.
Others were Pompooie, Fritzenpfeffer, Frieda von Gouldentitz,
Chef Peelsalotta Patatas, and, in apparent reference to his dairy
farming days, Fritzenmoo der Titzpuller.)

After Neil Gorse left town and moved to Thailand, Blank kept
in touch with him by email. Early on a weekday morning in June,
he sent this to Gorse: "Ahhh, no phone, no back doorbell, no
queries from the kitchen staff, no deliveries, no need to rush, and
a clear mind—the best part of the day for me. This week the Bravo
network has been running a really interesting series of well-pro-
duced, not overly political biographies, commentaries, historical
essays, profiles and flicks, including "Tales of the City" and a doc-
umentary about Fire Island, 99% of which was filmed in the Pines
[where they had had a house]. The cinematography was great and
made me sigh while recollecting fond memories, etc. Most of the
beach shots were directly in front of Beach Hill Walk, and the
boardwalk vistas were chiefly west of the harbor. Also shown were
the tea dance, the ferry coming and going, Tiffany's grocery store,
and various houses and households, including scenes of the typical
domestic quibbling over 'who's been eating my cookies,' and 'she's
such a mess and never does any laundry.'

"I watched 'Gladiator' recently, which was very long and very
real—the dirt, grime, squalor, rabble, slicing off heads, and such. I
guess the romantic, air-brushed, vintage Hollywood epics such as
'Quo Vadis' are passé (first dinosaurs, now Rome). Even the emperor

was raggedy-assed and worn looking. I nodded off several times.

"Well, dot's alles fur now. Pompooie."

Months after writing that, Blank received two pieces of startling news. In the course of bookkeeping, an unexpected sum of money was discovered in a restaurant account that made it possible to pay off the mortgage on the building. Blank now had equity to count on for his retirement. On top of that, an envoy from the University of Pennsylvania library system proposed an exhibition culled from Blank's personal collection. He wrote to me: "Semmel [I had been given a nickname of my own, a play on the common bread roll of Austria and Bavaria], Neil has returned from Thailand for a three-week visit. He is proposing that I retire and move to Thailand with him. That means I just sell the restaurant, lock, stock, and barrel. The mortgage is paid, so the only loss, in his view, would be that a major chapter of the Book of Life would end. He is negotiating for a new house, right on the beach, with the entire third floor reserved for me. Neil has never been one for sentimentality, so dismantling Deux Cheminées and all I have created here in Philadelphia seems just incidental activity to him. Unfortunately, I don't operate with such a matter-of-fact attitude. Ahh, the tears of us romantic fools."

With this came other signs that a certain cycle in the Philadelphia restaurant industry might be drawing to a close. On a spring night, the Garden Restaurant, in business for decades and where Esther Press McManus got her start, burned to the ground. For most of that time, owner Kathleen Mulhern had lived above the restaurant, but she'd recently moved elsewhere. When Blank phoned to offer his condolences, she said he was the only colleague from the Philadelphia restaurant community to call her. Around that time, a farewell party was held at the Four Seasons Hotel for Jean-Marie La Croix, one of the best liked and most acclaimed chefs in the city. When the hotel had opened in the 1980s, the owners were surprised by the success of its restaurant, the Fountain. Under La Croix, it consistently and sometimes successfully challenged Le Bec-Fin for top honors in the region. Success, however, did not keep the hotel chain from giving La Croix an early exit—to limit the size of his pension, in the minds of many observers. None of La Croix's chef colleagues were invited by the hotel to his farewell party, only business people and politicians, but Blank got wind of the event and crashed it. La Croix was so pleased to see his comrade that he broke off a conversation with the governor of Pennsylvania, a celebrated *fresser*, to greet Blank, kissing him on both cheeks in the Gallic way.

Soon Blank's turn came to be feted. On an October afternoon, in the Van Pelt Library of the University of Pennsylvania, the graduate in dairy science from a small agricultural college was honored at the opening of an exhibition titled, "A Chef and His Library." Michael Ryan, director of Penn's Annenberg Rare Books and Manuscript Library, addressed a room full of Blank's friends and admirers, many of whom had attended his classes at Deux Cheminées. "Few people associate cooks with books," he said. "We tend to believe that chefs are purely instinctive. But great chefs move forward by looking back. To collect is to harvest inspiration. People who make things taste good are also people of good taste. I have yet to meet a collector as genial and generous as Chef Fritz Blank."

A young friend of Blank's, Matthew Rowley, had assembled the exhibit, fitting a remarkable amount of information about Blank and his books into a compact display. "Blank's egalitarian collecting," he wrote, "embraces a range of culinary books from scholarly and esoteric to mundane and even downright tacky. Here, a 1627 banquet book written by a papal household steward shares billing with a 2001 Hooter's pocket menu and a cooking manual for Navy cooks."

The honoree, who seemed unimpressed by his new luster, ambled to the lectern and gave a talk he had titled "Old Recipes and How to Make Them Work." To recreate recipes from another day, Blank said, you must consider how ingredients might have changed over time, in measure or in nature. An old cake recipe, for example, might call for too much ground nutmeg, by today's standards. But in former times, nutmegs could have been years old by the time they reached market and their aromatic compounds dissipated, so cooks of the day compensated by using lots of it. Some ingredients, like celery, Blank said, have only recently come into general use. And the flavors of salted and smoked meat are less intense today than they were in the past.

After his talk, there would be ten more weekly lectures at the library, from Andrew Smith's social history of the Campbell Soup Company and its New Jersey environs to Steven Jenkins on the cheese business to Shirley Corriher on "Perfect Cheesecake and Beyond." Jessica Harris lectured, too, on Philadelphia as a Creole city. (She spoke not long after her mother died, and told me that Blank and her mother, Rhoda Alease Jones Harris, had talked often by phone: "They had a sweet relationship. My mother was always making lamb stew, so when she died, Fritz made lamb stew and sent it to me in New York for the reception after her funeral.")

The exhibition drew email from various quarters, which Blank enjoyed answering. "Regarding your query about 'A Chef and his Library,'" he told a correspondent at the University of Michigan, "there's not much literature associated with it. The U of Penn folks were very helpful in the arts and crafts department and provided money for the speakers, but producing companion notes and publications was not their shtick. (Of course neither did I have the time to produce these works, since my main job is 'peeling potatoes.') Still, the high-muck-a-mucks at Penn have praised the exhibit and pronounced it one of the best ever mounted within Penn's library complex (thanks in large degree to the designer, Matt Rowley.) The public response has been fabulous.

"There is a website. Go to www.library.upenn.edu/exhibits and click on Virtual Exhibits. As a lover of music, I have to say it's an honor to have my modest efforts in proximity to some really important collections in the music library of the Annenberg/Van Pelt Rare Books and Manuscripts building, notably the archives of Maestro Leopold Stokowski and the great spinto diva Dame Marian Anderson, lately joined by the effects of Maestro Eugene Ormandy and various other ephemera of the Philadelphia Orchestra.

"I was asked to do the exhibit not because I have a particularly large collection (~12,000 v.), or an especially old or focused one, but because my library reflects my personal avenues of interest in gastronomy. For Penn's part, 'my' exhibition was an experiment, if you will, part of an outreach program to reduce the university's hallowed, Ivy League mystique in the minds of the general Philadelphia community. Once again, the best way to the heart is via the stomach, or in this case, thinking and studying about the stomach."

Speaking of the stomach, Blank called one spring day to inform me that he was in the fourth day of a low-carbohydrate diet. "My doctor said it was either that or implant a shunt. I want no part of a shunt, so we'll see how the Atkins diet works for me." I wished him success, though, as I suspected, he wasn't able to lose weight and keep it off without systematic exercise. But I didn't raise the issue. I was pretty sure he would say he got enough exercise peeling potatoes.

Town and Country

*A*FTER THE CITY'S DECLINE from eminence, and before the revival in recent decades, Philadelphians who did not pull up stakes and follow the action elsewhere found comfort in private retreats. In town, that meant the Philadelphia Club, the Rittenhouse Club, the Acorn Club (for women), the Racquet Club, the Union League, etc. These were roughly analogous to the gentlemen's clubs of London, and indeed the Philadelphia Club, started in 1834, is as old as many of its London counterparts. Out in the mazy countryside, some club members took refuge on big estates with fanciful names, where they raised crops and livestock and rode to hounds. Upriver of the city, for example, on a hundred acres by the Delaware, lived a proud and numerous tribe named Biddle, who were financiers, diplomats, jurists, and high-ranking military men. A forebear in the shipping business, with family ties to Spain, had named their place Andalusia.

And then there was Androssan, about twenty miles west of Andalusia, where the heirs of Colonel Robert Montgomery (1881-1949), a founder of the Philadelphia brokerage of Janney Montgomery Scott, lived on six hundred acres of grazing lands named after a town on the Firth of Clyde. It would be hard to say which estate projected the most clout or panache. Old Nicholas (1786-1844), the most eminent of the Biddles, was a polymath who ran a literary magazine and, for a time, the Second Bank of the United States. James Biddle, a descendant, was president of the National Trust for Historic Preservation, and hosted evenings of cabaret in the library of the main house at Andalusia. Colonel Montgomery's grandson, Robert

Montgomery Scott—Bobby to nearly everyone—was president of the Philadelphia Museum of Art and an epicure of renown. But Androssan's trump card was the colonel's daughter (and Bobby's mother), the effervescent Hope Montgomery Scott, who was the inspiration for Tracy Lord, the character played by Katherine Hepburn in "The Philadelphia Story," and subsequently by Grace Kelly in the renamed remake, "High Society."

Many of the squires around Andalusia and Androssan took up fox-hunting, "the unspeakable in pursuit of the inedible," as Oscar Wilde put it. However unspeakable they might have been, these gentry knew edible from inedible, and aimed to eat well in their clubs and houses. According to Esther Press McManus, it was Bobby Scott who persuaded her to become the chef of the Philadelphia Club. And Nicholas Biddle so revered a caterer named Bogle (who was also an undertaker) that he wrote him an ode:

> *"Bogle! thou of Eighth, near Sansom, whose brow,*
> *Unmoved, the joys of life surveys,*
> *Untouched the gloom of death displays,*
> *Reckless if joy or gloom prevail—*
> *Stern, multifarious Bogle—hail!"*

According to Calvin Trillin, the Mencken of American eating, the food in private clubs varies by degree of exclusiveness: Quality declines as noses elevate. Putting aside Esther McManus's stint at the Philadelphia Club, I'm not inclined to question this, though I have no idea which clubs Trillin had in mind. He does not conceal his preference for crab shacks, sausage stands, and rib cribs over tonier places that provide plates and utensils, to say nothing of monogrammed table linens, backgammon boards, stewards in tuxedos, and, in the men's loo, old cartoons of cigar-smoking dogs playing card games.

It's likely that the Trillin theory was formed without considering two old and restricted Philadelphia clubs at which the members, and sometimes their guests, do the cooking. One of them, the

Schuylkill Fishing Company of Pennsylvania, also known as the State in Schuylkill and as the Fish House, was started in 1732. It is situated upriver of the city, though not, as one might suppose, on the Schuylkill River but on the Delaware, near Andalusia. Ancestors of mine, including a fox-hunting Quaker, were members. I have a history of the club, published in 1889, with penciled notations by my great-grandfather. "Their State," the book says, "is the oldest social organization speaking the English language. [The membership of White's Club, established in London in 1693, might wish to disagree.] Its members have, generation after generation, fished in the waters of our city's streams. They have all these long years of the growth in wealth and luxury of our nation preserved the same fare—the fish caught by their hands and served by themselves." I once saw a magazine article about the Fish House that had photographs of men standing about in aprons. I knew some of the men, but at that time in my life, before cooking took hold of me, I was not inclined to join—nor, I admit, was I invited.

The other do-it-ourselves eating club, called the Rabbit, was situated near the Schuylkill River. One February, friends who belonged to the Rabbit invited Risa and me there for a cooking party. She was visiting cousins in Vienna, Austria, at the time, so I went alone one Saturday afternoon to Belmont Plateau, near the city's western limits. Down a long drive, in a pine grove beside a golf course, I came to a modest bungalow covered in weathered wood shingles. Philadelphians are heirs to a Victorian back-to-nature movement, and they like their hideaways to be bosky and worn. The clubhouse of the Rabbit, said to date from the 1740s, fit that requirement. The uneven floor in the narrow front hallway creaked authentically when I walked in.

The host, David Sinkler, was there to greet me. "Here, hang up your jacket; you won't need it. And put on this apron. Do you want a drink? Becky's got a bad back. She's holding court from a sofa in the parlor." David had studied cooking with Esther McManus, so I knew I was in good hands.

I went into the small parlor where, from a couch, Rebecca Sinkler fixed me with her amazing blue eyes.

I said, "Too bad about your back. Does the pain have anything to do with the inauguration in Washington?" George W. Bush had recently begun his second term in office.

"No," she said. "The inauguration in Washington is the pain in my ass."

I made my way toward the kitchen, pausing at a chalkboard that listed the guests and their cooking assignments. I saw that I was on the soufflé team. This came as a mild shock because I had never made a soufflé. But I was cheered when I saw that one of my teammates would be the jovial and learned Bill Madeira; it was he who once told me about the funeral of an Old Philadelphian ("Maybe a Chew or a Cope, I forget") during which a nephew of the deceased stood in church to announce lunch following the service. "You will be glad to know," the young man said, "that we have several bottles of a really very nice Vouvray."

I looked around. The kitchen, in a shed-like annex on one side of the clubhouse, was ample but by no means fancy. It was slowly filling with people holding drinks and chattering. I was tempted to join them, but my kitchen work ethic, acquired at Deux Cheminées, took over. I rounded up the gear we would need on the theory that later on, we might be competing with other teams for bowls, whisks, and measuring devices. I found the menu and recipes, which David Sinkler had adapted from the *Joy of Cooking*: crab gumbo, roast butterflied lamb, garlicky spinach, and Grand Marnier soufflé with orange liqueur sauce.

By the time Bill Madeira arrived, I had separated the yolks and whites of thirty eggs. Together we zested oranges, using an antiquated grater I had found after a good deal of rummaging. The Rabbit's kitchen equipment bore dents and abrasions from many hands but functioned well enough to give the satisfaction one gets from a serviceable hand-me-down. Only an old Viking gas oven across the room caused worry when it belched and singed a woman's hair. Our soufflé production went into high gear when Nancy Davenport and Harry Groome completed our team. Eggs were whisked, heavy cream was stirred in, Grand Marnier was tasted and added, then went into the orange liqueur sauce as well.

When most of the cooking was finished, the gumbo squad bore its creation into the dining room, where we fell on it—thirty of us around a long mahogany table. I sat between two women, an educator and a realtor. We shouted affably at each other over our gumbo. Every course—plated, served, and cleared by the team that made it—turned out well, including the soufflé, which reached the table looking like pudding, or, as someone said, flan.

Toward the end of the evening, the table was cleared and its cover removed, the custom I had witnessed at Brasenose College, Oxford. No snuff was passed this time, but cordials were served, along with the last of the wine. Toasts were made and yarns told. Shyness allayed, I recited two of the Maine dialect stories collected and recorded by the late Marshall Dodge, a Philadelphian known to many in the room.

Several months later, Risa and I and her sister, Gerda Paumgarten, visited Jimmy Biddle at Andalusia to return some old family items. Off a leafy road just beyond the northeast city limit, we turned into a gravel driveway and drove on perhaps a quarter-mile beside fields and woods, past stables and ancillary residences, arriving finally at two big and dissimilar houses. To our right was the famous one, the original Craig family residence to which Nicholas Biddle had added a massive neoclassical facade. To the left, perhaps a hundred yards from the main house, was Jimmy Biddle's residence, all points and pinnacles in the Gothic revival style. Wide lawns with high shade trees ran down to the river's edge. The tide was up and the water choppy.

The squire of Andalusia was dressed for comfort in fawn-colored silk, with a brightly colored scarf at his neck. He was in his

70s, tanned, with sparse white hair, and he wore thin rectangular spectacles. After drinks we sat down to supper. "As you can imagine," Biddle said, "I'm always looking for ways to produce more revenue for upkeep here. At the moment I'm trying to track down the recipe for a curry powder that Colonel Alexander Biddle developed. The curry was rather famous around town, and I'd like to be able to make it here to sell in the gift shop. A pharmacist in Chestnut Hill claims to have the formula but says he won't part with it for less than thirty thousand dollars."

I said, "I know someone who might help you. He's a chef and a scientist and a food historian. Do you know the restaurant Deux Cheminées?"

"Yes, but I haven't been there in some time. I don't go to restaurants in the city much these days."

After supper our host walked us around the houses and grounds. In the library of the main house, we saw souvenirs of the friendship between Nicholas Biddle and Joseph Bonaparte, refugee brother of Napoleon, who lived for a time upriver.

Risa and I returned to Andalusia several times to attend the cabaret performances Jimmy Biddle arranged to raise money for his foundation supporting Andalusia's place on the National Historic Register. Performers came from New York, along with a number of Biddle's friends who enjoyed such occasions. We also went to a black tie subscription dinner at Andalusia to support the foundation that brought out a number of Philadelphia's old guard, in waistcoats and jewels. At some of these events, the dining rooms were illuminated entirely by candles.

I never discovered if Jimmy Biddle had consulted Chef Blank about the family's curry recipe, but one day, out of the blue, Blank told me he was spending time at Andalusia, consulting on menus. In fact, he said, he had planned the dinner for the upcoming annual fundraiser, which would be based on the recipes of the caterer Bogle, so admired by patriarch Nicholas.

Risa and I drove to Andalusia on a bitterly cold January night.

A dining tent had been set up on the south side of the big house. "Using the old dining rooms was too hard on the furnishings," an attendant told us. "Don't worry, the tent has been heated to seventy degrees." Risa was skeptical. "We'll see," she said.

We were invited into the library to see two horse paintings that Risa, Gerda and their brothers Harald and Nicholas had recently given to Andalusia. Their grandmother, Meta Craig Biddle, had spent her childhood in the house but was obliged to move into town after the early death of her father, ceding ownership of Andalusia to Jimmy's branch of the family. The paintings were among a number of family items Risa and her siblings had returned to Andalusia, including, from Risa, a pair of dancing shoes Jane Craig, her great-great-great-grandmother, had worn at her wedding to Nicholas Biddle in 1811. The library looked beautiful on this night, and the paintings were handsome enough, but the temperature in the room was too cold for lingering since the house had little artificial heat.

Cocktails went on for quite a while. Jimmy Biddle stood apart from the main scrum, and so did we after we encountered a puzzling behavior among some of the guests. One woman became noticeably chilly to us when she learned of Risa's connection to the Biddle family. Soon after, when another matron responded the same way, we chose anonymity.

"My ex-husband was related to the Cadwaladers," said the woman seated to my right at dinner. "I think he had some Biddle cousins, too. And what brings *you* to Andalusia?"

I said warily, "I'm a friend of the chef who planned this dinner. He's a food historian, you know."

"Oh? How nice." She turned away and did not speak to me again. Perhaps the temperature had affected her mood. Our table was in a corner, close by a gap in the tent side and far from any source of heat. Shivering guests retrieved their overcoats from the house and wore them for the rest of the evening.

We had entered the cold tent expecting to eat, but first we listened for an hour to Broadway tunes sung with skill and gusto by a baritone from New York. Then came our reward: fish soup with bits of halibut, wassail (spiced wine), veal breast stuffed with vegetable purée, and Brussels sprouts with *sauce bâtarde,* and, for dessert, *crème caramel.* As the dinner concluded, Jimmy Biddle gave a short speech and thanked Blank for his participation. The chef stood to acknowledge the applause. In his brown corduroy jacket, he looked like a poet among oligarchs. He came to our table and took the chair recently vacated by my piss-elegant neighbor.

"In a few days I'll be going to the Pennsylvania Farm Show in Harrisburg," he said. "I've been asked to give some cooking demos, and, of course, I can't say no. I love the Farm Show. And nobody in tuxedos."

I was well aware by then of Blank's affection for rural Pennsylvania. We had traveled together to Lancaster County to visit Betty Groff, an expert on Pennsylvania German cooking. And Blank and I had gone one July to the Kutztown German Festival, where we ate fried chicken and ham with mashed potatoes, chow chow, apple butter, *schnitz und knepp* (apple dumplings) shoofly pie, and milk tart. Blank called it "all starch and gravy" but not in a complaining way. We inspected quilts (one had been auctioned for more than $5,000) and antique farm machinery, and Blank bought sleigh bells and hand-decorated eggs. It was a happy day for him and an occasion when his girth did not make him conspicuous among the farm folk.

Blank wrote to his email list, "Hi !! I will be in Harrisburg doing cooking demonstrations during the week of the Pennsylvania Farm Show. As you may know, my first college degree was a B.S. in dairy husbandry. I am delighted that agriculture and family home cooking are still important parts of what makes the U.S. tick. You might see me on the Pennsylvania Public TV station. I am always surprised to get calls from Philadelphians who watch this farm-oriented TV station."

Risa and I drove to Harrisburg to see the Farm Show for ourselves. As we sat in traffic outside the vast and swarming exhibition complex, I was inclined to believe the notion that Pennsylvania has the largest rural population of any state. Inside, we dodged our way to an enormous food hall. Friends, including Blank, had praised the Farm Show baked potato, a steaming spud heaped with butter. It met expectations, and the rest of the show was even better. I believe we saw every variety of farm creature, from Angora rabbits to Yorkshire swine. Anyone who could not find at least one specimen of horse, pig, cow, sheep, goat, rabbit, chicken, duck, or alpaca to admire would have to be severely agri-phobic.

We found Chef Blank at the Culinary Connection, the largest of several cooking demonstration stages in the exhibit halls. He was wearing his white tunic and English toque, the Swabian butcher's outfit, as I now thought of it. Nearby booths promoted maple syrup, garlic, and the state lottery. A slow country waltz played on the public address system.

"I'm in pain," Blank said. "The insides of my thighs are chafed raw, and my entire crotch is inflamed. I didn't bring my cellulitis medication, and the farm show doctor can't write me a new prescription. He recoiled in horror when he saw it. I applied Bag Balm, but no relief. I don't know how I'll get through the milking contest."

"Milking contest?"

"It's something Betty Groff started years back. Teams of celebrities, so-called, compete in relays to see how much milk they can get from a cow in the allotted time. Neophytes and veterans like Betty and me—it's a mixed bag, pardon the pun."

Blank carried on gamely, leading us behind a curtain at the back of the demonstration stage to show us a large prep kitchen where Betty Groff was bustling about.

"I'm nervous about the contest," she said. "Last year, the handler washed my cow's teats at the wrong time and threw off the release of the milk, so my team lost to Fritz's."

"Don't worry," Blank said. "This time I might not be able to kneel to milk."

We accompanied the rival captains to a small arena where two teams of four formed up. Groff gained the advantage when the

Pennsylvania secretary of agriculture was assigned to her team. He was an agile-looking fellow who, I was told, grazed five hundred head of Holstein on his seven-hundred-acre dairy farm. Sure enough, the Groff side produced eleven ounces of milk in the time allotted to the Blank team's five. I winced as I watched him shuffle painfully to his cow and kneel, though once in place, he looked masterful. It was too little too late, unfortunately.

Back at the Culinary Connection, Betty Groff showed a large and rapt crowd how to make corn and oyster pie and sweet potato pie, including the crust. ("Use butter. Why be a farmer and use margarine? You don't know what's in it.") Blank, sitting to one side on the stage, contributed information about varieties of sweet potatoes and yams.

"I'm all the way from Mount Joy, Pennsylvania," Groff said. "I've been doing the Farm Show for twenty years. Fritz and I are distantly related. At least we like to pretend we are." I thought of the many connections Blank had established beyond his little realm in Philadelphia—from Oxford, U.K., to Oxford, MS; and from Andalusia and Androssan to Erice; St. Andrews, N.B., to Mount Joy.

Jimmy Biddle died at Andalusia in March of 2005. He was seventy-five. Risa and I went to his memorial service and sat near Bobby, who was in a wheelchair. Bobby died in October of that year, at the age of seventy-six, in a hospital not far from Androssan. "An enduring legacy" and "quintessential Philadelphian," the newspapers said of both men.

Some months later, I visited Blank in his library office. The morning was cold, and a space heater was going for the benefit of BoBo the cat, who slept in a basket near him.

"I've been thinking about the tradition of gentlemen farmers keeping dairy herds," he said. "Jimmy Biddle kept Guernseys, descendants of a herd that Nicholas brought over. Bobby Scott gave the Ayershires he had at Androssan to my old school, Delaware Valley College. His mother kept about three hundred head and named every one of them. Speaking of Bobby Scott, look at that." He pointed to a bookshelf nearby that held a row of ring-bound notebooks. "They're drinks recipes, compiled by Bobby's father, Edgar. Bobby offered the collection to me one day when we were both visiting Jimmy Biddle at Andalusia. Apparently, Edgar Scott employed a secretary but didn't have much business for the secretary to work on. So he thought of recording everything he knew about mixing drinks. As you can see, it was quite a lot. Bobby said to me, 'What's a rich man with a secretary to do?'"

19.

Blank Unbound

W HEN BLANK SPOKE of his future, he would often say, "some day when I stop peeling potatoes." He meant, of course, some day when he was free of running a top-drawer French restaurant with two-dozen employees on the pay-roll. (Most mornings he did, in fact, peel potatoes, along with lots of other prep work). But when would that day come? And when it came, what would happen to Deux Cheminées? And where could Blank go with his huge library?

Now and then he would tell me of places he was considering for retirement. One candidate was Molunkus, Maine, a town beside a lake of that name where his parents had taken him as a child. An-other prospect was southern New Jersey, where the two of us had traveled to eat muskrat and some of his cooking class alumnae lived. He also thought about retiring in the Pocono Mountains, about two hours north of Philadelphia.

Gorse had gone ahead with his own plans, building a house on the Gulf of Thailand in what Blank described to me as "an enclave of expatriate wealth." His friend's absence from Philadelphia did not help Blank's general disposition. Nor did episodes of bad health. Several times he called me from a hospital room to say he had been admitted for sudden complications of diabetes. "The trouble is," he told me on one of those occasions, "humans are being kept alive beyond their natural lifespan." Yet, in body or mind, he never seemed to stay down for very long. "I come from good peasant stock," he would say. Thirty years of grueling restau-rant work testified to that.

When Gorse, still trying to persuade him to retire to Thailand, invited him to visit, Blank accepted with misgivings. What if he liked it there? What if the retirement bug hit him hard? "I can't imagine leading Neil's indolent life," he told me before he left.

He spent three weeks in Thailand one January, a slack time at the restaurant. "I was up every morning at five to write in my journal," he said when he got back. "Then I went to the beach around nine and usually got a massage. You can also get a manicure and a pedicure. The children gave me an affectionate nickname that means 'Fatso.' They would rub my belly and even kiss it for good luck. It's a nice life, but I don't know if I'm ready to vegetate in that way."

It was a time of his life, though, in which Gorse and Thailand (or, rather, Gorse and the *food* of Thailand) won Blank over—that and restaurant burnout. The spring after his visit to Thailand, he attended the biennial conference of food scientists in Erice, Sicily. When he got back to the restaurant, he told me, "I walked through the door, breathed in, and thought to myself, 'Who needs this?' I called Neil next morning and told him. He said I could come stay in Thailand for the summer."

That summer Blank wrote cheery postcards from Thailand, often embellished with droll squiggles. (He had a talent for cartooning.) "Life is sweet!" he wrote. "The food is five stars—it's simple, with a never-ending cascade of flavors, textures, colors, and aromas. Chilies are an important ingredient, and so is sour stuff. The more I explore, the more impressed I become." There were emails, too: *"Sawazdee! Sabei Dee?* Translation: 'Greetings! Are you well?' This is just a note to let everyone know that I am well and that I do miss Philadelphia (sort of) and my friends, and my kitchen and staff at The Doo. I also miss BoBo the cat. The weather has been hot, but on the beach, it's very pleasant, and the constant breezes off the Gulf of Thailand are cool and delicious. We lounge in beach chairs under canopies of umbrellas, served by staff who provide food and drink and most anything else. My quarters in a new complex are very comfortable, although I am using a

small, very basic kitchen until the main kitchen is designed and installed. The garden is lush and full of tropical botanicals. Of course,
I am welcome to visit Neil's beach house whenever I want, and I
keep my bicycle there and peddle every day about 2/3 of a kilome-
ter to our preferred section of the beach. The cost of living is *very*
low compared to stateside prices. Thais are extremely hard workers
and take pride in everything they do. This includes the Boyz Boyz
Boyz set. Life is a beach!"

His return to Philadelphia and the restaurant brought Blank the
usual crush of duties, including his cooking classes. On a Monday
in February, his topic was hors d'oeuvres—profiteroles, shrimp
mousse, deviled crab casserole, stuffed mushroom caps, and mussels
steamed in white wine and buttermilk. "In my recipe collection,"
he said, "hors d'oeuvres are the second most numerous, after cookies. People tend to use store-bought appetizers, but you can make
your own, in quantity, ahead of time and keep them for more than
one occasion." He showed us how to use an implement he called a
shark to scoop out mushrooms and other vegetables suitable for
stuffing. And he gave us a recipe for batter made with beer or
Champagne ("It can be used for almost anything—fish or vegetables, even pickles"), cautioning us to season fresh vegetable oil for
deep fat frying. "You have to heat it, cool it, and then heat it again.
Otherwise it can be bitter. Whatever you do, don't use canola oil.
'Canola' is an acronym from 'Canadian oil low acid.' I hate it."

Days later, Blank staged his annual dinner-musicale to raise
money for the Philadelphia Singers. He had been conducting these
events for more than a decade now, and with the help of friends
and a few generous suppliers, had raised thousands of dollars for
the worthy but often cash-strapped organization. The honored
composer this time was Beethoven.

"Tonight's meal represents what Beethoven might have enjoyed
when dining at home," Blank wrote in the menu notes. "He often
preferred eating alone and favored simple peasant dishes prepared
by a housekeeper. One of his favorite evening meals was *eintopf*

Menu covers from two of Chef Fritz's many benefit dinners at Deux Cheminées for The Philadelphia Singers, featuring foods that might have been served to the composers in their honor.
2006 (Beethoven), 2004 (Berlioz)

('one-pot'), a rather pedestrian soup or stew that he sopped up with bread. This might have been accompanied, or followed, by a piece of Parmesan cheese. With this he usually drank beer."

Blank's version of Beethoven's supper was anything but one-pot. Of the seven courses he served us, from *Huhnebrühe Mit Leberspätzle* (poultry soup with liver dumplings) to Viennese goulash to *Apfel Streudel,* my favorite was the soup. ("Only the pure in heart can make good soup," Beethoven once said.) The dining rooms were filled with concert habitués, including Christoph Eschenbach, principal conductor of the Philadelphia Orchestra. Risa and I sat at a communal table in the front dining room, a sanctum with leaded windows, wood paneling, and flowered wallpaper that reminded me of the *beisln* of Vienna. The Singers performed three times during the meal in the big entry parlor. Sound was piped into the dining rooms, but several of us, including Blank, went to the parlor to watch and listen. Where else in the realm of highbrow kicks, I wondered, might one eat *Forelle im Teig mit Haselnüsse* (batter-fried trout with toasted hazelnuts, our third course) and then hear, impeccably performed, "Bonny Laddie, Highland Laddie," a folk song Beethoven composed for a Scottish patron?

And yet, as the saying goes, no good deed goes unpunished. Several days after the Beethoven dinner, Blank was shopping when he tripped on a curb and fell, spilling the bag of groceries he was carrying. "It was very embarrassing," he said. "I couldn't get up. I was right across from Esposito's, where everyone knows me, and people came running out to help. My knee still hurts."

Another physical problem had to be dealt with a few weeks later when he had an operation for accumulated plaque in his coronary arteries. A catheter was inserted near his groin, and in two places where the arteries required widening by angioplasty, wire mesh stents were placed to keep the sites open. Afterward, he felt much better. He emailed friends, "My heart is now in tip-top shape. Most all the barnacles are gone, and I feel like a new person. I now face retirement with a refreshed attitude." Indeed, when I next saw

Blank, four days after his "barnacle" procedure (he was serving fried chicken and potato salad in a church anteroom after a Singers rehearsal), his face had better color than before—not the familiar red flush or the sallowness of recent months but, you might say, the palette of good health.

The change that Blank had been contemplating for years began to unfold. On May Day 2006, less then two weeks after his stents were put in, I climbed the worn stone steps of Deux Cheminées to attend the chef's final class. I had been his student for ten years, going frequently in the early days, then less often as business demands increased. While topics naturally varied from class to class, the tone and structure of "In the Chef's Kitchen" remained comfortably the same, from Blank's digressive chitchat in the foyer to breakfast in the staff dining room to the main act, the chef cooking and quipping before twenty or so amateur cooks.

On this melancholy occasion I arrived well in advance of the other students and went down to the kitchen. Blank, the early riser, was already in full fuss, in company with a staff dishwasher and white-jacketed volunteers, Lisa and Pete. Today's centerpiece would be ballotine of chicken—birds boned, stuffed, and rolled before roasting. I put on an apron and worked on breakfast, making toast and stirring a double boiler of Blank's buttery scrambled eggs.

He would leave in a few weeks to spend three months in Thailand, the longest holiday of his working life. He returned to work in September and then, the following June, retired from the restaurant and moved to Thailand for good. Blank was to have a happy ending to his restaurant career, so it seemed, though not all his friends were happy on his behalf.

"Ken Cundy phoned me early this morning," he said. Though Cundy could be a high-strung nuisance, Blank was invariably kind to him and his wife, Alice. "Ken fell yesterday and broke his hip. I don't get it. He's nearly deaf and Alice is getting forgetful, but they won't move out of their big house, which they can't manage. Now this. Ken complained to me for half an hour, and when I told him I had to go get ready for class, he got mad and hung up. Other people are behaving strangely, too."

"You're important to them. They're upset you're going away."

"Jeez."

We went upstairs to join the class gathering in the lobby. Blank took his place at the reception desk, and I sat on a couch under the windows. I had never taken that particular seat before and did so now for the view it gave me of the reception rooms, all gilt and oil paintings and chiming clocks. Not many years before, my family's old house had been sold and its contents dispersed. Some of the loss I felt then came back to me now.

Blank passed around a dish of peanuts he had roasted and flavored with five-spice seasoning. "It's asparagus season," he said. "If you're going to steam or grill asparagus, you can make it greener on the plate by soaking it first in a solution of three-quarters teaspoon of baking soda to a gallon of water. I never get tired of asparagus. Here we prepare it in advance by cooking it in the convection oven. Then we shock it in ice water to stop the cooking process. To keep it warm, we put it in pans that we slide under the stoves. No, the sliding it under the stoves part is a joke. We just warm the asparagus before serving it."

All the students went downstairs to the pantry and crowded around the chef as he deboned a chicken for the ballotine. "It's not a quick process but worth learning because the principle is the same whether it's a duck or a pig or a lamb. Like everything, it gets easier with repetition. I once deboned twenty turkeys for a dinner of the International Association of Culinary Professionals. It was enough for three hundred people."

We followed him into the kitchen where he mixed stuffing in a big bowl with his hands. We were given a taste of the cranberries which had been soaked in *kirschwasser*. They were bracing, to say the least. From years before, I remembered Blank's cherries soaked in Calvados and grieved that this man with the protean palate would be leaving town for good.

Blank stuffed and trussed several deboned birds, wrapped them in cheesecloth, and put them in a convection oven. He then made whipped cream for a mousseline, pouring a third of a cup of cold heavy cream into the mixer bowl, to which he added a generous teaspoon of granulated sugar and a pinch of salt. "Use table salt here for the finer crystals," he said. *"Fleur de sel* and kosher salt will dissolve differently on the tongue." After three minutes or so, he added another two-thirds cup of the cream. "This will keep for about five hours at room temperature."

"So," he asked, "what sauce would you make to go with my stuffing?" There was silence followed by a few mumbled replies.

"Chocolate?" someone joked.

Blank said, "How about a mushroom-shallot reduction with cream and a bit of thyme?"

"My second choice," said the joker.

Blank took one of the chickens from the oven, ran a trussing needle into the center, pulled it out, and touched the tip of the needle to the skin below his lower lip. "This is the most temperature-sensitive part of your body, at least when you have clothes on. This needle is cold, so the bird needs more time."

The mousseline was for the asparagus. To the whipped cream, Blank added grated orange peel, the restaurant's own mayonnaise, and Gran Torres, an orange liqueur from Spain. If he had thought of it, he said later, he might have included some orange marmalade.

While trying to keep track of Chef Blank's instructions, I also wrote down nonessential things, husbanding memories. I noticed for the first time a big openwork rubber mat on the tile floor in front of the stoves, a leg saver, no doubt, for a chef with bad knees. Through the back of Blank's tunic, I read the promotional inscription on his T-shirt: "Nuts to You" and "www.nuts-to-you.com."

The chicken was taken out of the oven once more and judged to be ready. "I should let it sit for a bit," Blank said as he sliced the bird, "but we're running late. I guess I should have done the deboning last night." We didn't mind, not wanting the class to end. As he sliced, I understood what the fuss was about over ballotines and gallotines: They were savory versions of the ice cream roll, all tender meat and stuffing, no bones to contend with. "Good for picnics," Blank said.

As class ended, one of the men stood (the number of male students had increased over the years) and made a short speech thanking Blank on our behalf. We applauded. Blank seemed pleased and at a loss for words. He retreated to a chair by the big pantry table where members of the class said goodbye to him. "I guess it really hasn't sunk in that this is the last class," he said. Back in the kitchen, with the chef's permission, some class members were wrapping up unused food to take home, including entire chickens. Blank had always been liberal in this way. When pharmaceutical companies gave dinners at Deux Cheminées for physicians and other clients, guests were sometimes allowed to take home entire roasts. Without permission but without guilt, I filched my own souvenir, the recipe printout for Blank's sweet whipped cream. "For some unknown reason," he had written on the sheet, "this recipe is little known to chefs and American homemakers."

So Blank had settled on a place to retire, but what of his books? One evening that spring, he and I drove to the Asian market complex in South Philadelphia. We wandered a while in food aisles that smelled of fish and pickled radish. Blank happily surveyed bins of voluptuous produce. "If I start to buy something, stop me," he said. We had not come to shop but to visit a Vietnamese soup stand that served pho, a beef broth flavored with star anise, ginger, and coriander. As we bent over our bowls, Blank talked about disposing of his library. In order to cook and write about cooking, he said, he would need some reference works at hand. But transporting fifteen thousand books overseas was obviously out of the question. He would have to find a home for most of his collection.

"Barbara Wheaton came down from the Schlesinger Library at Radcliffe and drooled over some of the rarer books," he said. "Penn seems to want the pamphlets, which have anthropological value. The Restaurant School tried hard to get the entire collection, but I turned them down because they have no graduate program, just chef trainees who have no time or inclination to read. So we'll see. Next year, when I retire for good, I'll pack a shipping container with the books I can't do without, and then I'll try to find a home for the rest."

Blank left for Thailand at the end of May. Two weeks later, he emailed friends in North America and Europe:

"I am happy to report that all is well here. Neil is fine and dandy, and I am happily renewing acquaintances with the people I met last year. My new kitchen, which Neil designed, is simply *wonderful!* It's very spacious and well equipped, with a large central butcher's block table and restaurant-sized appliances. There are lots of cabinets and a wall of windows that look out on a woodlot filled with interesting birds and mammals. It's all quite perfect and should prove to be most suitable for recipe testing. I am putting the finishing touches on a paper I will present at the Oxford Symposium in late August before I return to Philadelphia and my kitchen duties at Deux Cheminées in mid-September. I will spend the early part of January in Harrisburg at the Pennsylvania Farm Show, and I should like to sponsor one last Composers Dinner as a fundraiser for the Philadelphia Singers. Then sometime next spring, I shall officially retire as Chef de Cuisine of Deux Cheminées. I will remain listed as 'Chef Propriétaire' but will reside permanently in Thailand on a retirement visa. I must confess I already miss my many friends in Philadelphia, especially my fellow workers at 'The Doo.' I also find myself looking about expecting to see my cat, BoBo, meandering about and keeping me company. I'll write more as the summer progresses. Meanwhile, I send my best wishes and regards and hope that everyone is in good health and enjoying life's many gifts.

"Here is a short vaudeville recipe for your amusement and/or groans:

Gracie Allen's Recipe for Roast Beef

1 large roast of beef

1 small roast of beef

Take the two roasts and put them in the oven. When the little one burns, the big one is done.

—Paw Kru-ah (That's phonetic Thai for Papa Chef.)

I visited Blank one afternoon late in the year, after his return to Philadelphia. He was seated at the big table in the staff dining room, preparing fennel and Italian parsley for *sauce vierge.* He got up from chopping the parsley with a Chinese cleaver, and hugged me. He had shaved off his mustache and goatee.

"I don't know why I'm here," he said. "The staff doesn't listen. I tell them to cook a fish *en papillote,* but they don't want to take the time. Get 'em in, get 'em out, boom boom." As if to illustrate Blank's complaint, the line chef appeared in the doorway, wearing street clothes. A party booked for that night had canceled, Blank told him, though he wasn't sure how many they were. The chef turned to leave, but Blank called him back to say that a friend who ate at Deux Cheminées the other night thought his fish was over-done. Put the fish in at the last minute, Blank said, after the salad is ready; it doesn't need much time in the pan. The chef had been cooking for years, and no doubt was pained to be corrected like this. He listened, nodded, and walked away. "I'd be happier if I were in Thailand, not here," Blank said. "I'm perfectly content puttering around my house. I don't get brain farts the way I do here. For in-stance, what the hell have I done with my *sauce vierge* recipe?"

"It's right here in front of you," I said.

Early in 2007, the year of Blank's retirement, the University of
Pennsylvania announced it would acquire his library. "Penn's Rare
Book and Manuscript Library houses many rare treasures," the
campus newspaper said, "but in its stacks you'll also find 'Quick
Cheese Tricks Using Kraft's Cheez Whiz.' The brightly colored
mid-twentieth century pamphlet is part of the vast culinary collection of Chef Fritz Blank, longtime chef/owner of Center City's
romantic Deux Cheminées restaurant. Blank, who taught classes
for Penn for sixteen years through the College of General Studies,
plans to pull up stakes this spring and retire to Thailand. He will
take maybe a hundred books with him. The rest—around fifteen
thousand print and manuscript cookbooks from the seventeenth
through the twenty-first centuries—will come to Penn to join the
roughly three thousand promotional pamphlets and community
cookbooks the library acquired in 2005. . . ."

At the time of the earlier acquisition, Blank had stressed how
honored he felt, as a music lover, to have his "modest efforts" close
by the archives of Marian Anderson. Now, for his final dinner musicale to benefit the Philadelphia Singers, he chose to honor the
great contralto from Philadelphia, two days before the 110th anniversary of her birth.

"Will the menu be Southern?" I asked.

"No," Blank said. "She had a very sophisticated palate."

What was unsophisticated about Southern food? I wanted to
ask. But I held my tongue.

For this, our last meal at Deux Cheminées, Risa and I were given
a table precisely where we had been seated our first time there
eleven years before. This time we were in company with Blanche
Burton Lyles and Phyllis Sims, respectively the founder and the
curator of the Marian Anderson Historical Society, based in Anderson's former home in South Philadelphia. "Blacks in her day

couldn't go out anywhere," Sims said, "so everybody, especially in South Philadelphia, had their basements fixed up. She put in a bar—her favorite drink was Champagne—and some furniture and a piano." I reckoned Marian Anderson, who died in 1993, would have been pleased by this musicale in her honor, in the home-like surroundings of Deux Cheminées, scarcely a mile from where she had lived. She certainly would have been gratified that Blanche Lyles, her protégé, had purchased the Anderson family house to preserve it for posterity. A pioneer in her own right, Lyles was the first African-American woman to perform a piano recital with the New York Philharmonic at Carnegie Hall.

In early spring, Blank dispatched this emailed announcement: "TAG SALE FOR FOODIES. After a lifetime of collecting, and as I prepare to retire to smaller quarters, it has become necessary that most of my household of books, kitchenware, furniture, ephemera, memorabilia, tableware, and other assorted 'things' and collectables be managed and dispersed. The bulk of my culinary library is being donated to the University of Pennsylvania, including my personal papers and various collections of food- and hospitality-related items (menus, magazines, special events, restaurant and hotel collectables). Nevertheless, there are still lots and lots of items that I cannot keep after retirement. So I am preparing an On-Premises Tag Sale on May 26 and 27, 2007, Memorial Day weekend.

Partial List of Items for sale: French copper cookware (a large selection), slow-cookers, bain-Maries (like new), electric fry pans (like new), cake pans, pie pans (both glass and tin), mixing bowls, terrines, jars, and small cooking tools of all sorts. A large assortment of collectables and quality knick-knacks, including cow statues, pig statues, eggcups, decorated eggs, beer steins (glass, porcelain, and stoneware), coffee mugs, bookends, cookie jars, animal miniatures, miniature liquor bottles (lots), food-related calendars (lots), food-related postal cards (lots), crystal: (cocktail, highball, and old-fashioned glasses, plus candy bowls, candle chimneys, sugar and small mint bowls, salt cellars, and other service pieces, fruit and nut bowls, a crystal wine bucket, and more); white serving ware (pitchers, bowls, terrines, pasta plates, small fluted brioche candy dishes, and more; furniture (living room and dining room, bookcases, divan, sideboards, trolley, chairs, rocking chairs, desks, sandwich high tea server), and more stuff yet to be listed."

Weeks before the tag sale, word went out that the restaurant itself was for sale. The asking price, according to the *Philadelphia Business Journal*, was $3.95 million, including kitchen equipment and furnishings for the front, the liquor license, and the rights to the name Deux Cheminées. Blank told the magazine he had no regrets about selling the restaurant or offering its name to another restaurateur. "I don't care," he said. "It's not copyrighted. I won't fret."

I was surprised, in fact, by the equanimity of the self-described nester in the face of such dramatic change. In addition to the restaurant he had created and nurtured, he had spent years filling the upper floors of a former men's club with his effects—keepsakes, curios, and *objets*, as well as books—and now was willing to let it all go. In those final days, only some bureaucratic pother over a visa for himself and health documents for BoBo, his cat, seemed to ruffle Blank's feathers.

I was surprised, too, by how well he brought off the enormous dispersement, though I needn't have been. Blank was always a good organizer, and he was not shy about asking friends for help; when the call went out for assistance at the tag sale, I volunteered with about a half-dozen others, most of whom had attended Blank's cooking classes. Principal among them was Patricia Arcaro, a lawyer and accomplished cook who had studied with Blank from the beginning.

The tag sale was scheduled to begin Saturday morning at seven. When I arrived at the restaurant not long after six, prospective buyers were camped by the side door. Blank was down in the kitchen, working. The restaurant was still in operation, and would stay open until the 8th of June.

"Go upstairs and pick something out for yourself," Blank said. I did. I prowled around the library for a few minutes and came across a simple, handsome oak box, big enough to hold five-by-seven-inch recipe cards. I took it to Blank.

"That was my mother's," he said. "I'm glad you chose it."

"Did she use it?"

"She only used recipes when she was baking. Because in baking, as you know, you have to be precise. Wait. Change that. I mean you have to be accurate, not precise. There's a difference. You can measure out precisely without being accurate. That could happen if the instrument you're using is off." I was getting a cooking lesson at six-thirty in the morning. What would become of my culinary education once Blank was gone?

When the sale began, at least fifty shoppers were lined up at the side door, which gave access to the stairs leading to Blank's quarters on the second floor, where the sale was held. Most seemed in a good mood, including the first arrival, a Mr. Gutman, who bought copperware, books, and memorabilia—perhaps two-dozen items in all. I thought he might be a dealer, but he told me he was just looking for mementos. Blank moved among the crowd, greeting well-wishers, answering questions, and discussing the provenance of various items. Two enormous Hungarian dining chairs were a gift from Louis Szathmary. A set of Limoges china came from the house on Delancey Street that Blank and Gorse once shared. "No chips, no breaks, even though we had a glass-topped table," he said. By afternoon, the surge of buyers had subsided, and I was able to do some shopping of my own. I cast a wistful eye at the Hepple-white-style bureau in Blank's bedroom, which had matching veneers and a marble top, and I admired a fat art book, with recipes, about Henri Matisse and his life and work in the south of France. In the end, I bought a few pieces of silverware from the Delancey Street days, some porcelain cows that appealed to me, and *The Pine*

Barrens, by John McPhee. The New Jersey Pine Barrens is an enormous sandy tract in the heart of the state that is sparsely populated and little known to the outside world. Late in life, Blank's parents had moved there from Pennsauken. He had encased McPhee's book in a plastic cover, the way public libraries do.

When I returned the next morning for Day 2, I noticed a sign on the front of the building: "Sale: Fully equipped restaurant with liquor license."

"We were scrambling at turn-out last night," Blank said. "A lot of staff took the weekend off. It felt like the old days, back when we opened."

Upstairs, there was a Sunday morning mood. Only a few buyers had come early. To avoid being enticed by unsold items (I had my eye on some coasters from the Raffles Hotel), I went down to the side entry on Camac to meet new arrivals. In the lulls, I inspected the awards displayed in a hall nearby. They were from the AAA (four diamonds), Mobil (four stars), the James Beard Foundation, *Travel Holiday, Gourmet,* and *Wine Spectator*—nice enough, I thought, but they hardly did justice to the chef the Zagat Survey had called "a national treasure."

I said goodbye to Blank that evening, knowing we might not see each other for several years. We hugged and exchanged some pleasantries. Then, microbiologist and pedagogue to the end, he held forth briefly on the digestive process of elephants, apropos of a box of notepaper sitting on a nearby table.

"This paper was made in Thailand from elephant dung. Elephants aren't ruminants. They don't chew their cud the way cattle do, or sheep, goats, camels, and so on. More than half of what they eat comes right out the other end, undigested, which makes them very good processors of cellulose for paper."

In the final days of Deux Cheminées, many tributes came in. My favorite appeared on eGullet: "my gf and i went last night for a first and final dinner (closes for good on friday). it was our joint birthday treat to each other (sounds better than 'going dutch') so we got all dressed up. we had a perfect experience. great food and drinks, perfect service, got to meet and chat with the chef afterwards."

Blank reported from Thailand, "The Thai-Air flight to Bangkok was wonderful—no problems whatsoever. *And* BoBo was a perfect passenger. She did not cry or meow the entire journey, including the hours we spent en route from Philadelphia to JFK, the wait in the airport, the flight itself, and the car trip from Bangkok to our new home. Door-to-door the trip took nearly twenty-four hours but was more comfortable than I had imagined. Once here, BoBo soon became the Queen of the Castle and is quite happy in her new digs. And so am I.

"I continue to discover the pleasures of authentic Thai cuisine that can be appreciated *only in situ,* consumed al fresco, native style, out of communal bowls with fingers, a soup spoon, and fork. (Chopsticks are not Thai!) Lots of smiles and lip-smacking celebrate the simple bounty of a family meal here.

"I do miss Philadelphia, especially my long-time friends and, for sure, my connections with Penn, Monell, the orchestra, the Singers, and old Deux Cheminées regulars. PS: All eighty boxes of my stuff arrived on the doorstep yesterday morning! I shall unpack slowly. I've got plenty of room and plenty of time. It's sort of like Christmas in that I don't remember a lot of what I packed, so each box is a surprise. BoBo sniffs everything to certify that it is from 1221 Locust Street.

"Please keep in touch

"FCB"

Index

About the Author

*S*AMUEL YOUNG has been a writer, editor, publisher, photographer, and photography editor, principally for magazines. His work has appeared in *Holiday, Travel Holiday, Town & Country* and *Connoisseur,* among other publications, on subjects ranging from food and travel to art, architecture, music, and the paranormal. The latter interest resulted in *Psychic Children,* a seminal book in the field, first published in 1977. A Harvard graduate, Young lived in New York, Umbria, Austin, and Philadelphia before moving to Albuquerque, where he resides with his wife, artist and designer Risa Benson. He remains an avid cook, thanks in large measure to the tutelage of Chef Fritz Blank. In recent years, he and Benson have taken up Argentine tango, a pursuit Young finds nearly as complex, inexhaustible, and rewarding as the world of gastronomy.

Made in the USA
San Bernardino, CA
12 September 2014